Praise for

Un-Doing Conditional Love:
Life Lessons in Love, Loss, & Forgiveness

Pam Miller has written from her heart. In *Un-doing Conditional Love,* she shares moving "Wisdom Stones" and offers wise life lessons that can help you live in a greater state of unconditional love.
—Marci Shimoff, author of NY Times #1 bestseller *Happy for No Reason* and *Chicken Soup for the Woman's Soul*

Pam artfully captures her life lessons and offers them to the reader with humor and graciousness. *Un-Doing Conditional Love* will be helpful to anyone who is going through or has already traveled through life's many losses and is looking for a reason to believe again.
—Lorna Dobson, author of *I'm More Than the Pastor's Wife: Authentic Living in a Fishbowl World*

Un-Doing Conditional Love is extraordinary! It releases us from reactivity, frustration, and judgment of both ourselves and others. It then grows our depth of peace, joy, love, and happiness. Pam Miller is a gift to her family, her friends, and multiple businesses and clients around the world. You will appreciate her sharing and teaching as you read this book. It is a gift to us all.
—Rhanda Salameh, Therapist, Coach, Business Consultant, Energy Healer and Spiritual Mentor

In *Un-doing Conditional Love*, Pam gives us a glimpse of experience in caregiving for a loved one with ALS. Pam understood the journey. Her moment by moment, description of life inside ALS is real. Before, during, and after the disease. I highly recommend this book and the gift of presence Pam shares with all of us!

> —Deborah Gelinas, MD, Founding Director, ALS Center and Director, 2008-2014; Clinical Neuroscience Research at St. Mary's Healthcare; author of *Living with ALS: Managing your Symptoms and Treatment*

Un-Doing Conditional Love allows readers a glimpse into the world as seen through Pam Miller's eyes—a world full of possibilities where love comes without limits and conditions. Pam's words and big heart allow us to truly understand what it means to live from the perspective that life doesn't happen *to* us, but is always happening *for* us.

> —Kasey Mathews, Transformational Life Coach and author of *Preemie: Lessons in Love, Life and Motherhood* and *A Mom's Guide to Creating a Magical Life.*

Pam Miller's story of losing her husband is one that many, like me, can relate to. While acknowledging the heartbreak, Pam comes alongside the reader and offers profound understanding and hope for the healing journey, as well as simple ideas for making life better right away.

> —Grace Liang, Gracefully Grieving Energy Coach; author of *Finding Grace: How to Navigate the Journey from Tragedy to Triumph.*

Pam Miller has a way of tackling tough material and life challenges head-on, with courage, and from a place of love and compassion for self and others. She walks the walk and truly embodies a spirit of taking responsibility and facing her fears. *Un-Doing Conditional Love: Life Lessons in Love, Loss, and Forgiveness* is a roadmap and a companion for those who are navigating through grief and loss.

>—Khursheed Sethna Ph.D., author of *Free Your Spirit Find Your Voice: Be Seen. Be Heard. Be Believed!!* Speaker, counsellor, and Inside Out Voice Coach.

I laughed out loud, I smiled, and shed some sentimental tears!
>—Pam Van Dyke, R.N

UN-DOING CONDITIONAL LOVE

Life Lessons in
LOVE, LOSS, and FORGIVENESS

PAM MILLER

Copyright © 2020 Pam Miller

All rights reserved. No part of this book may be reproduced in any form or by any electronic or mechanical means including information storage and retrieval systems, without permission in writing from the author. The only exception is by a reviewer, who may quote short excerpts in a review.

Cover designed by Barbara Martin, 99 Designs

Photograph by David DeJonge Studio
Visit his website at www.dejongestudio.com

Illustrations by Jayne Small
Visit her website at www.jaynesmall.com

Pam Miller
Visit my websites at www.pammillerconsulting.com
and www.undoingconditionallove.com

Printed in the United States of America

First Printing: July 2020
Kindle Direct Publishing

ISBN: 978-0-578-71178-2

DEDICATION

To my family.

Whom I love UNCONDITIONALLY.

CONTENTS

Acknowledgments   xi

Introduction   xii

PART ONE: Unconditional Love

1. Family   1
2. Many Neighbors, Many Churches   7
3. Deer Camp   11
4. Vacation   15
5. Becoming Blended   19

    Reader Reflection: *Unconditional Love -* 24
    What Does it Mean to You?

PART TWO: Loss

6. Little Livia — 29
7. ALS — 35
8. The Present: Gifts of a Caregiver — 41
9. Legacy — 47

Reader Reflection: *Loss — What Does it Mean to You?* — 51

PART THREE: Forgiveness

10. Finding Forgiveness — 59
11. Living Life — 65
12. Spiritual Gifts — 71
13. Knowledge + Wisdom — 77

Reader Reflection: *Forgiveness — What Does it Mean to You?* — 80

The Wise Woman Stone — 84

About the Author — 85

ACKNOWLEDGMENTS

Many who knew me asked to share my story of ALS. I was always willing to speak to people one on one or groups as well. I never thought I would put it in a print form because the task seemed too difficult. This book would not be written without the support and belief in me from so many. The list is long, and I could not leave out any one of the people below.

I thank you, Jack Canfield and Marci Shimoff, for mentoring me, believing this was my time, my way, of reaching many with similar life stories. Your support meant so much, and guided me to my writing coach, extraordinaire, Kasey Mathews, and my brilliant editor, Dr. Marilyn Montgomery.

Kasey, you accepted me as a newbie, and yes, I know I challenged you more than once. How you knew to get my words out of my head and on to the page was sheer genius. I am forever grateful for instilling in me the enjoyment and impact of the written word.

Marilyn, when I learned of your expertise and your willingness to take on my book, my gratitude went deep. You have made this book make sense and made my words flow. The editing you give is a gift and a blessing; I am very fortunate to have you on my team.

One of my best sounding boards, Sarah Storck, read the very first scribbles of chapters and has stayed in the game to see this book to fruition. Thank you for your loyalty.

The love and support from my cousin, Patty Tuliper, who has faced loss herself, listened, and comforted me. I hope I did the same when you needed it. You are a treasure.

To my husband, JJ Bouma, who carved out an adventure with me in our life story, I will never forget you or the love we shared, for you are with me.

To my husband, John Miller, I thank you for daring to love again with me when our lives changed. Adventures can still happen, and we have more memories than most.

INTRODUCTION

I wrote this book of memories and life lessons for those of you who may have similar experiences. I hope it brings you back to stories of your own—stories of joy but also, maybe, great pain; stories of loss and stories of learning, but all stories that have made you who you are. Or you may bring to this book a wish to change pieces and parts of your life and to make sense of the future.

Wherever you land on the spectrum, I want you to know that tomorrow is a new day—a day in which you can choose to give, find, or receive unconditional love.

You may be a parent, caregiver, or simply an individual who feels stuck in life due to your circumstances and decisions you made some time ago. Or you may have a sense of living through a story more far-reaching and significant than just yourself. Or you may feel really lost, asking yourself, "Where do I go from here? How can I move two steps ahead without falling back, one or more?"

I've taken on the responsibility of raising and guiding children, even when they are not of my own blood. Looking through the prism of a mother's eyes, I share my insights on how to succeed at blending a family. I learned that making things conditional—in other words, extending my love only when certain conditions were met—was the wrong road to jog down. The "conditional" road is a road where pain and struggle exist.

I've taken on the role of caregiver, and as I learned what it meant to be in that role, I chose to love more powerfully and unconditionally than I had ever loved before. I survived the losses in my life and came out on the other side whole again.

I've taken on the role of a grieving spouse, determined to make my husband's legacy a reality. But it was a road I walked alone. Through the weeks, months, and years after the passing of my husband, being alone was difficult and tested my faith in the future. I learned, however, that we are not alone, even when the mind and heart would say differently.

I now try to keep my thoughts and my awareness in the present. Learning to do so has been my saving grace. Staying in the present is a daily – even hourly— discipline, but it has gotten easier to make it part of my daily routine. However, I did not arrive at this point of grace without experiencing grief, loss, and love as I knew it.

In my moment of deepest pain, my sadness from losing my true love, I realized that a veil of grief was lingering over my face. It was keeping me from seeing clearly, and from being truly seen. I realized I needed to move myself out of that place of darkness; a place where I only felt sadness; a place I hope never to have to go to again.

So, I studied. I read, and I practiced what I read. I interviewed people--hurting people--who understood my story and wanted me to listen to theirs. I walked alongside those who doubted whether they could continue to put one foot in front of the other. With every encounter, I learned. I learned a way to live life at peace with myself and the world. And what I learned, I am sharing here with you.

The event of my husband's illness happened. The response I chose to the event of losing him, and all that it meant, ultimately determined my life outcome. Today, my life outcome is not being a victim, but a victor.

Do you feel stuck? Welcome! You've come to the right place. I share some of my "Wisdom Stones" to take with you. Give them a home and return to them often. Hold them in your heart, even when it feels like your heart has a hole in it that doesn't seem to heal.

Are you single? Or miserable in your current circumstances, thinking that life isn't fair? I share with you the stories that led me to my outcomes in this book. When we are alone, we are more prone to believe that if we can just *change* (our hair, our attitude, our weight—you name it!) then love will find us. But this lie—that love will happen when we re-arrange our conditions—only leads us to find *conditional* love.

Conditional love and condition living are very toxic to the body and the mind. Conditional love emphasizes limitations and restrictions, whether due to actual incarceration or to the invisible walls you have built to protect yourself from hurt. Conditional love keeps fear in place. Real love is on the other side of fear.

Use this book to reflect on your own experiences of love—both conditional and unconditional. Use it to face and embrace your losses, too. In the "Reader Reflections sections, you'll see places where I ask you questions. I've given you space to write your answers and reflections. Think of us having a conversation and trust the words you find yourself writing on the page—they'll lead you forward!

Forgiveness—especially forgiveness of yourself—will allow you to set yourself free and live a life of unconditional love. Dare to step through the veil of fear. Join me on the journey. When you do, you will ask, "Why did I wait so long?"

Part One:
UNCONDITIONAL LOVE

CHAPTER 1

FAMILY

Family is the most important thing in the world.

—Princess Diana

Gray dust billowed behind the tires on the dirt road that seemed to stretch for miles. Dad sat in the passenger seat with Rick at the wheel. A driver's training permit and the dirt road to Grandma and Grandpa's farm was just the right way to get experience.

"Watch going over this hill for other cars and stay on your side of the road," Dad said, pushing on the pretend brake on his side. He seemed to be in control of the car.

I rolled down the window in the back seat, tossing my hair every which way. "Watch, Mom," I said, putting my hand outside and letting the wind dip it up and down without my help. The sun came through on my face, bright enough to make me close my eyes.

"Are we almost there yet, Mom?" She could tell I was ready to get out. She smiled and said, "Almost!"

"You better slow down a little bit, son, to make the turn in the driveway." Rick sighed at Dad's suggestion and hit the brakes. The farmyard was full of cars, and that meant a lot of cousins around. Mom was the oldest of nine children in her family, and we were there to have Sunday dinner together.

"This is going to be a great day!" I started squealing from the back seat. Now beginning to jump up and down, I yelled, "Stop the car, Rick, I want out." I waved at my cousins while hanging halfway out the window.

Dad turned around in his seat with a direct stare. "You stay put, young lady, until this car comes to a complete stop, and the key is out of the ignition!"

"Yes, sir," I said, sitting down on the seat.

My cousins were so much fun and being able to play together at the farm was very special. At last, I jumped out of the car. "Let's go to the barn, girls," as I motioned them to follow me. Playing in the hayloft made an excellent spot for a hiding game.

"Watch out for the new kittens just born. Grandma told me to remind you not to pick them up; they are too young yet to be away from their mother," Mom called out. We had already started across the yard to the barn. Once inside, Deb, Gwen, and I climbed the wooden ladder attached to the cross beams of the hayloft.

"SHHH, be quiet! I hear them crying ... listen!" Deb said. Sure enough, mama cat and her litter of kittens were between a couple of hay bales.

"It's OK, mama; we won't take them," whispered Gwen. "Look how tiny they are! And they sound hungry, too."

We all sat very still watching mama cat snuggle in to feed her babies. Grandpa always said that barn cats have great importance on the farm. So, we decided to leave them alone to grow up. Mama cat would teach them everything they needed to know.

The barn's main door opened, and out came a clopping noise. Old Topper was Grandpa's swayback horse, going for a walk with Grandpa, who loved giving rides to the grandkids.

"Who wants to go first?" Grandpa asked as he stopped Topper by the corral fence. All three of our hands went up at once. "Climb up on the fence and get on, one at a time, behind each other. All of you can ride together," he said.

"I have the longest legs, so I'll sit at the back," I offered. The other girls agreed with me.

"Now sit up close to each other and hold on, so no one falls off." Grandpa's rules made us all giggle. The feeling of warmth on my legs felt so good, riding bareback rather than with a saddle. Topper's ears and tail twitched as he knew the exact timing to keep the buzzing flies away from his body. Grandpa muttered concerns about the old boy, speculating whether Topper would make it through another winter.

"Let's go, Grandpa," Gwen said, grabbing onto the mane. Away we went, holding on to each other while Grandpa and Topper talked together in their own language.

We got a couple of laps around the yard when the long line of kids waiting began shouting, "It's our turn now!" We reigned in Old Topper to a stop and carefully got off.

The old screen door slammed behind me as I entered

the kitchen where Grandma had just finished baking the pies for our dinner. "Smells great, Grandma!" *That one must be the apple pie*, I told myself.

"Pam, will you go down in the root cellar and get two jars of dill pickles for me?" Grandma asked.

"Sure!" I replied. "You know they are my favorite." She smiled at my answer.

The root cellar had an original set of stone steps that went along the outside foundation of the house. The smell of an earthen floor and cold stone walls greeted me when I reached the bottom level and opened the wooden door. The only light was a bulb that I tightened in its socket so I could see. My eyes adjusted to the soft light to see rows of glass jars on shelves.

"Wow, just look at all of this," I whispered to myself. Grandpa and Grandma went through a lot of hard work for this food. Red beets, green peas, yellow corn, peaches, and pears were perfectly canned and stored. The strawberry jam on the top shelf was a family favorite; noticing it took my memory back to the time Grandma was bitten in the foot by a rattlesnake while picking strawberries in the field. A feeling came over me. It was peaceful... along with a great sense of gratitude for what it took to preserve all this for the upcoming winter.

Mom met me coming in the door. "Here are the pickles," I said.

"Dinner is just about ready," she said. "Go tell the kids to wash up before we eat." The back door slammed again as I went outside.

The steam was rising off the biggest bowls of mash

potatoes and gravy I had ever seen on the dining room table. Placed next to them was a platter piled high with fried chicken. "Are those your chickens, Grandpa?" one of the cousins' asked.

"Yes, some of the plumpest ones I have ever raised," he proudly said, rubbing his hands together and reaching to pass the platter of the best his farm had provided. It was a feast that took many hands to prepare. With genuine pride and thankfulness, gazing at the whole family at his table, he proclaimed, "EAT UP!!"

"I'm stuffed to the gills," I moaned later. The last piece of pie was left in the kitchen for someone who still had the room for it. No one ever went home hungry from here!

I had the most loving family that anyone could ever want. And I knew not everyone had one like mine.

Mom and Dad

It was Monday morning, and all of us had to leave the house on time. Rick and I went off to school, and Mom and Dad to work. "Good morning," sang Dad, as I plopped down in my chair to eat breakfast.

"Mornin." That was the best I could do.

Rick turned to me and said, "Why so grumpy?"

My brattish answer: "None of your business."

"Geez!" Rick muttered as he shook his head at me.

"Why are you in your Dress Blues, today, Dad? Must be pretty important," I observed.

"When your career is the United States Marine Corp,

you wear this uniform sometimes," he replied. "Like when I have to attend meetings with Government officials. But today I have to be in a parade downtown."

"You look very handsome, honey." Mom replied, with a quick kiss to his lips as she delivered the eggs and bacon in front of him. Our parents were never embarrassed to show affection to each other, like hugs and kisses. We received the same.

Rick grabbed his books. "I'm out of here," he declared, and out the door he went. He was getting to drive his car to high school, which was too far away to walk. It also allowed him to skip school on occasion! Geez!

"Eat your breakfast, or you will be late for school. Hurry up, or your friends will leave you behind and you'll have walk alone, sweetheart." Mom needed us all out the door so she could get ready for her ride downtown. She worked in retail as an assistant manager of a major department store. She was the only mother in our neighborhood who worked away from home.

When I had to bring a treat–say, for my birthday—she always made the cupcakes the night before. She put Rick and me ahead of herself, no matter how tired she felt. I hoped I could be just like her when I grew up and was on my own. I was so proud of her and what she accomplished, even without higher education! Yet, as a Mom, she wanted much better for her children.

"Are you working late tonight? If you are, then Dad and I can pick you up," I offered.

"Yes," she would reply. "Your TV dinners are in the freezer," Perfect! *Easy and straightforward*, was my thought. *Turn on the oven and stick them in. Oh, and set the timer!* My cooking skills came from watching my Mom in the kitchen, but I had never stepped up to be the sole cook for the whole family.

Brother Rick

My brother Rick was always (deep down) my hero, growing up. Even though sibling rivalry was alive and well at our house, life's moments kept us close.

"Mom, I can't take Pam's teasing me anymore!" he'd yell, running after me into the kitchen to seek refuge in my Mom. "Can I hit her just once, so she will leave me alone?" he'd ask, slapping his hands together.

"No, you cannot. You are six years older than she is, and she will get hurt," Mom responded, turning from the stove. I looked up at him from behind the safety of her legs. Rick stood 6'6" as a teenager and had a pretty good reach when he wanted to catch me. I stuck out my tongue at him, knowing I deserved his wrath more times than not.

The neighbor girl was going ice skating. "Do you want to go along?" she asked. "A lot of kids are going to be there. We can give you a ride." Of course, I accepted.

Walking out of the house with my skates on, I announced, "I'm leaving my boots home, so I don't have to change when I get to the pond." Sliding into the back seat of their car, I heard my friend say that her Dad would drop us off and pick us up in a couple of hours.

It was a bitterly cold day, and after an hour, I realized I didn't have warm enough socks on. My toes started to hurt from the cold. I stopped skating and waited for the ride to come. It didn't. Soon, tears ran down my face.

I finally asked, with a hollow sound to my voice, "Have we been forgotten?" It was starting to get dark.

Just then, my friend shouted, "He's here; come on, let's get you home." I tried to stand up from the bench when I realized I had no feeling in my feet. The pain was gone, but it was hard to move and get into the back seat of the car.

"Dad, hurry up and get Pam home; her feet are frozen!" When the car pulled up in the driveway, Rick came out to the honk of the car. He took one look at me, sobbing my eyes out.

"It's OK. I got you," he said reassuringly, bending down to pick me up in his arms.

"I can't walk or feel my feet!" I cried, burrowing my head into his shoulder.

"Then let's go inside and get you taken care of," he replied, more calmly than he no doubt felt. He sat me down on the bathroom counter and said, "I have to get these skates off your feet, and it's going to hurt some. Do you understand?"

I nodded. "Yes, I guess."

After both skates were off, I looked at my pure white skin and swollen toes. They looked like baby sausages. Still crying, my eyes met Rick's and I asked, "Am I going to need my toes cut off?"

He put his arms around me and held me close. "No, they need time to warm up. That's all." He drew water in the sink that was cool, not warm. "Now dip your feet in a little at a time." The pain got worse as they started to thaw. After about an hour, he dried them off and carried me to the couch in the living room.

"I'm still c-cold, Rick," I stammered, shaking with chills.

"I know; it will take a little while for your body to heat back up," he replied, piling more blankets on to get me warm. It took me two more days before I could walk normally again. But after that, I never forgot what the depth of a brother's love felt like inside my heart, knowing he would always be there for me.

I dare say my teasing him also stopped!

CHAPTER 2

MANY NEIGHBORS, MANY CHURCHES

I am love.

—God

As a child, the block we lived on was lined with houses full of children, all close in age to me and my brother. This was a sign of the times in the 1950's, after the war. Every night there was a ball game in the back of someone's yard. When it got dark, we played hide and seek and kick the can for summertime fun. Sleepovers with the neighbor girls was a weekend event that I loved. A lot of good stories told in the dark meant a few hours of lost sleep, which was part of the deal!

Church was significant in our community, most families regularly attending every Sunday and holidays. One of those churches was directly across the street from my elementary school. It had a wonderful after school program every Wednesday, where any of the children from the public school could go for lemonade and cookies.

When the school bell rang, my classmates and I would hurry down the hallway toward the exit. Once outside, a group of us broke off and walked to the crosswalk that would lead us to the big brick church with a beautiful white steeple on the corner. I'd tap my foot on the curb, waiting to cross, always excited to get there and watch a fun Christian-themed story on a movie screen and sing some hymns. After the movie and singing, we'd go into our individual classes, which were sorted by school grade, and listen to the teacher read stories from the Bible.

One of my best friends, Debbie, and I started Kindergarten together, so we were in the same class in church school. She lived a street over on one side of me, and her Grandparents owned the dairy on the other road behind me. The best ice-cold chocolate milk in little glass bottles ever was one of the production lines! Her dad worked there and would often share a bottle with each of us when we went to visit after school. What a treat! Her family were also members of the church.

We started our walk home together after church school was finished. Crossing a couple of yards and streets I began to mimic the piano lady while running my hands up and down a keyboard in the air, then I would take a bow, and both of us would laugh like crazy. We also did a little "twist and shout" that certainly wasn't allowed in the church.

Thinking about that day's lesson, I asked, "Debbie, what did you think about the forgiveness talk today?"

"Well," she said while kicking some stones down the

side of the road. "If you did something wrong, you need to ask God or the person to forgive you."

"Saying you're sorry is pretty easy," was my response as I shrugged my shoulders. "Why do you think people hold grudges?" was my next question.

Her answer is something that struck me deeply. "I think it's because some people think they are right, and the other person is wrong, as simple as that."

I looked at Debbie and said, "I hope they talk more about it next week. It seems to me that too many people are making it hard to forgive!"

It was during those after school church programs that I first witnessed anyone other than adults praying out loud. I'd watch my friends bow their heads and take turns reciting prayers among the circle of students. I'd feel my palms start to sweat, and I'd panic over my lack of Christian education and worry that I didn't know how to pray correctly out loud. I'd do everything I could to get out of the oral prayers.

And yet, I knew the love of God and prayed silently with all my heart. I just struggled to put it into words for others to hear. In that sixth-grade moment, I thought all the other girls were so smart because their families were members of the church. I so wanted to belong just like the other girls. But because as a family, we didn't have "membership papers," I thought I was missing out.

So, I became the girl in the neighborhood who went to church with all the other families. I'd go to the Reformed Church with Debbie's family, and the Christian Reformed Church with the Marshalls, the Lutheran and Methodist Church with our neighbors down the street and the Catholic Church that had huge stained glass windows, with my cousin Patty.

Every week, I'd find a way to get one of the girls in the neighborhood to invite me to their church and then their Sunday School. I loved going to all the different churches and seeing how each Sunday service went. Some were the same length of time, and other ministers went on forever. That's when you could look around and see a few people dozing in the pews! But the thing I noticed was that no matter which church I was sitting in each Sunday, every single one talked about the message on God, salvation, and love. Some spoke about fear too.

I never dared to bring up religion at home. My parents were perfectly fine with me being invited to other churches and always asked what I had learned that day. My mother had been baptized at age twelve, and I knew it was something that someday I would commit to as well.

But there seemed to be a rule at our dining table...which was never to debate religion or politics. The conversation was never deep when the subject came up. I knew that my parents attended church throughout the years in the military on the base they were stationed at when I was very young. But somehow, as I grew up, whenever I asked why we didn't go to church, my dad would simply say, "We try to live by the Ten Commandments, love God, and our country. You'll find it in the Bible on the bookcase." I knew what he meant because that is how our family lived our lives... end of discussion.

So, I kept going to services with the neighborhood families, noticing how each one of these churches followed their own ways and rules, just like in our home. I loved paying close attention to the differences between the pastors, ministers, or priests and their manner of speaking as they delivered the message to their congregations. Their personalities ranged from serious to humorous, and I did have my favorites.

Sitting on the hard pew benches, keeping my back as straight as possible. I'd slowly suck on the mint my friend's mom had slipped us, listening and working hard to understand the meaning of all that I was hearing. I hoped the same stories will continue next week...when I got a chance to attend again!

CHAPTER 3

DEER CAMP

Now then, get your equipment—your quiver and bow—and go out to the open country to hunt some wild game for me.

—Genesis 27:3 NIV

I sat curled up on the living room chair, looking out the picture window, enjoying the falling leaves that had changed into the brilliant reds, oranges and yellows as they do every year. Fall was my favorite time of year. It was the season I was born in, and I knew Mom would be making me a chocolate birthday cake with thick chocolate frosting. She would invite my girlfriends from school to celebrate with a party. As always, hoped for some new clothes for my Barbie doll as presents.

I learned very young that there are seasons within a season. Deer hunting was one of them. The November calendar was upon us and many family members were gearing up to head to deer camp. I observed early on that getting ready to go away for a week takes lots of planning. I'd watch Dad and my older brother Rick lay out all the right equipment to assure success in the hunt. They always threw in a few decks of cards to play with my uncles and cousins while in camp. Cousin Jim and Steve had a way of winning a lot of cards games. As the stories would go, some were better at poker than others! Oh, how I wished to be part of the fun!

Dad allowed me to go to the shooting range and watch them practice before the hunt. He always made sure the sights on the guns were perfect. For me, being around firearms was very natural. Dad was a drill sergeant when he was in the Marine Corps; later, he was on the rifle and pistol team and competed around the world. My brother and I had gun safety drilled into us along with the respect it takes to own a firearm.

Dad always said, "Owning a gun is a privilege and responsibility." After shooting practice, we'd go back home and clean the rifles on the kitchen table.

Dad and Rick would talk about the moment a big buck would step out of the thick brush and Dad always spoke very seriously about how the buck would give his life as a sacrifice. It was very important to preserve the meat that would feed our family and many others. Reverence was a natural part of preparing the deer for the journey home.

Dad and Rick always wore the bright red coats and hats in accordance with the hunting regulation laws so they could be seen from a distance and not be mistaken for a deer moving in the woods. Pretending I'd be invited, I'd put on my favorite coat—Dad's big heavy wool red and black plaid coat. As I strutted around the house in it, the weight of it pulled my shoulders down and it covered my knees at the same time. The deer hunting license was attached on the back, inside a plastic pouch, held with a giant safety pin. I couldn't wait for the day when I would have a hunting jacket of my very own.

When the day came to pack up all the gear, Mom put a bunch of meals in the bottom of the cooler in the back of the family station wagon. "Chili is the perfect camp food," she would say, and she always made a huge pot of it. She'd also made a cake, a pie, and a few dozen cookies that were staples for my brother's extreme sweet tooth. My mouth watered, just looking at all the treats and wishing I was going too.

"Well, we're ready to go." Dad announced. Rick made final checks on the sleeping bags and pillows. Family vacations were very special, no matter where we went together as a family. But hunting deer on opening day in November was father-son time, and they both looked forward to it as very special.

"Dad, how come I can't go?" I'd always ask. Every year I hoped it would be the year I was old enough for him to take me.

"Sorry, honey," he'd say, with a pat on my head. "Deer camp is for boys only." It was always the same answer, but I never gave up asking, year after year. I wanted to hunt and harvest a deer. Being a girl didn't seem like a good reason to me for not being invited.

"You and Mom will have fun together," Dad would say, and then kiss us both. Mom and I would watch as he and Rick pulled away and the car left the driveway. We would wave until the car was out of sight.

Mom knew how hard this was for me and always tried to cheer me up. "Let's have something fun for dinner tonight," she'd say. "Anything you like. You pick." But I was never hungry.

Because I was a girl, I was stuck at home and missing the adventure of deer camp. It always took a couple days for me to get my appetite back. Mom never seemed to take it personally. She understood.

So, for the next week, we would go shopping for school clothes and go out to eat for hamburgers, French fries, and my favorite, a chocolate shake. I know Mom enjoyed not having to cook big meals every night, but for me, it was just one of the ways to pass the time and distract me from thinking about where I really wanted to be.

I kept myself occupied a couple of days raking the fallen leaves. I'd start by making leaf piles as high as I could. My prize was a soft landing spot when I jumped on top. The leaves made a crunching sound when I laid back on them for a rest.

A cool fresh breeze always came to blow the next round of leaves across the yard. I watched the sky. It was so deep blue with the largest white puffy clouds. I wonder where the clouds would go from here. The nature of our world always intrigued me—especially the seasons, as they never stop changing, including hunting season.

Dad and Rick's return from deer camp was such an exciting time. All the hunters would tie their trophics to the front fender or roof of the car. When hunters were traveling home, others would pass the car and give the thumbs up, honk and wave on the good luck!

This year, Dad had gone into the nearby town to call us with the news before they left for home. He had taken his big eight point buck this year! He had seen him last year, but never got a clear shot. Rick took a doe with his tag and was very excited. The thrill of the hunt was something I had always longed for, someday I'll get the chance!

"Here they come, Mom!" I squealed as the car drove up the driveway. There it was, strapped to the top of the station wagon and looking to be as long. When the car stopped, Dad got out, just in time to catch me jumping up with my arms and legs wrapping around him.

"Wow, what a beautiful buck!" I couldn't help my enthusiasm. I jumped up and gave my dad the biggest kiss on the cheek.

"Big doe, brother!" was my next commendation, tossed over my shoulder. Rick had pride written all over himself as he stood by his trophy. Still in my Dad's arms, I asked, "Are you going to get it mounted?"

Dad put me down and said, "Yes, this one needs to hang on the wall!" As he untied the big buck from the car, he laid it on the driveway. Then he said, "Sit next to him and I'll take your picture." This was a tradition that was all mine for as far back as I could remember. I was the first one to be part of the hunt...back home.

I crouched down on my knees very close and grabbed the antlers, then held the majestic head up high. I could feel my smile—so big, looking right through the middle of the buck's rack as the Polaroid camera clicked, taking the picture. Waiting for the photo to develop, I realized that in some way, I was part of Dad's deer camp, even though I wasn't one of the boys.

When I do grow up, I resolved, maybe Dad can be part of *my* deer camp someday.

And it won't be for just girls!

CHAPTER 4

VACATION

My father gave me the greatest gift anyone could give another person. He believed in me.

—Jim Valvano

A trout stream was the usual summer destination for our family. And fly fishing was the Holy Grail in a blue ribbon stretch of water.

In our family, we were campers; the kind that were a step up from tents. We were always up off the ground and had a solid roof over our heads. But everything else was primitive. No running water or electricity. We loved the outdoors, and spending time there was a way of life.

"We are the only ones here, Dad," I remarked as I looked through the trees.

"Yes," he replied. "Nice to have the whole riverbank to ourselves. The water level is down on the river and you know what that means—great fishing."

I jumped out of the back seat of our car with my best

friend, Pam, following me. Mom knew I would have more fun if a girlfriend was sharing the trip, since Rick was off and gone from the house.

"Don't forget the dog, and make sure you keep him on a leash." Mom ordered. Hans was a beautiful cinnamon color dachshund and my first very own pet.

"Come here, boy!" I called taking a hold of his collar.

"He can't go too far with those short little legs," my friend Pam said with a smile.

Well…" I countered, "He just about lost his happy home this summer by chewing our kitchen doors to pieces. Puppies chew, and he was the worst," I proclaimed, as I recalled my "bad dog" story.

"Remember when you ran away, the night they told you they were giving Hans away because of all the destruction?" Pam reminded me. "You know you were very lucky to have your parents forgive you AND let you keep the dog."

"I know, that was the worst thing I ever did to my parents," I confessed with remorse. "I was so sorry I scared them that way. I'm still really, really sorry for scaring them like that." Just thinking about that night, my eyes welled up with tears again. Hans looked up at me with his big brown eyes then pulled me by the leash to the nearest tree to get relief from the long ride. Then off he ran for a drink in the river.

"Girls, I need your help unpacking the car and setting up camp," called Mom. "OK, we'll be right there. Let me tie Hans up first to the tree."

Dad grabbed the old fold-up army shovel and headed away from camp to dig a hole between two trees. A sitting board went between them, and then he stretched a tarp around it. "Ladies, your bathroom awaits." He bowed with a big smile on his face.

Mom waved him off with her hand, sighing, "Oh, Rodger."

The other job to be done was hunting for firewood. We cooked most meals over charcoal, but breakfast was usually prepared on the Coleman stove. The collection of wood sticks for the campfire needed to last each evening. Hiking along the trails that stretched back and forth in the trees was a good place to find them.

At dinner that night Dad shared our fishing plans. "Tomorrow morning you girls are going to paddle me down the river in the canoe so I can fish."

Pam and I looked at each other and said together; "Uh, what??" We both liked to fish from the bank and go on hikes, but never had we paddled a canoe together, let alone have someone fishing from the middle seat.

"You will do just fine. Mom will pick us up at the next bridge downstream. It should take about three hours to float that distance." Again, both of us looked at him, thinking, what are our chances of tipping over? In our estimation, they were off the charts.

"You just need to keep us going straight down the river, watching out for the dead fallen trees. That's what can tip us over. Besides, I know you can do this," Dad said reassuringly.

"Such confidence he has in us," Pam said, as we both burst out laughing.

Shrugging his shoulders, Dad's favorite line came out. "Well, you're not going to learn any younger."

Mom rolled her eyes at us all, then said. "Life jackets, for sure, on all of you." As we went off for adventure, whether at home or in the woods, she was always the one to say, "Now be careful." Not with a fearful voice, just concern with common sense sprinkled in.

The evening was over, and Dad put out the campfire and we all went to bed. Hans was stretched out between Pam and I and didn't budge all night.

I woke to the sound of Dad rustling around and peeked outside. "Beautiful day," remarked Dad, enjoying the smell from the first pot of coffee being brewed on the outdoor stove. He was such a morning person—the military in him, I think.

I peeked at my fried Pam, still asleep, then pulled up my sleeping bag over my head and closed my eyes again. On vacation you had permission to sleep in a little while longer.

After breakfast, Dad announced the plan. "OK, girls, I think we need to pull out around ten o'clock this morning. Then we can be back at camp around lunch time."

"I'm wearing my swimsuit so I can try to get some suntan." Pam said, and I agreed. The chances of us getting wet was on the high side.

"I packed you some snacks so you can stop and take a break in the shallows." Mom offered us a small cooler.

"Stop?! Do you think these two will know how to stop the canoe when they need to?" Dad said, teasing us.

"You're the one that has all the confidence in us, so I hope you're right," I laughed back at his comment.

Now here is where it gets tricky. Both me and my friend were named Pam. Dad was trying to give us instructions on how to paddle, calling out "Pam" every time he gave an order. He lectured us on how to stay out of trouble; admonishing us to be in perfect control when he had a fish on the line so that he didn't lose the fish.

"This is going to be a crazy ride, Dad," I observed with both excitement and doubt. "

Yes sir, it is going to be crazy," my friend Pam echoed, and we both burst out laughing.

I took the rear seat in the canoe, only because I had some experience paddling with my brother. Pam had never been in a canoe, but she was game. As we pushed away from shore, Dad's fishing pole came out and the casting began. At the same time, the canoe made its first complete circle in the middle of the river. After we had the tipping thing under control, we all started to relax a bit. But as we reached the first bend in the river, the circles continued.

Mom waved to us from the shore, shaking her head yelling, "Good luck!" She had to be wondering if there would still be three people in the boat when she picked us up.

Pam and I giggled and laughed like teenagers do. Dad never got mad at us, not even once. The only time he gave us a command was to stop the canoe because he was fighting a very large rainbow trout on his line. "I don't want to lose this one, girls, so back paddle now!"

Well, around and around in a circle we went. "You two are something else!" Dad pronounced, laughing as hard as we were.

"We are trying Dad, really, we are!" we squealed.

The big fish got away, but fortunately Dad didn't seem too disappointed. Zigzagging down the river, we eventually made it back to shore. We never got soaking wet. But Mom did teasingly ask us, while standing on the bridge and watching us come around the last bend, if we were dizzy. As Dad got out of the canoe, he announced, "That was one of my best fishing trips ever!" We all burst out laughing again while dragging the canoe out of the water.

That night, sitting around the campfire, the stories of the day grew bigger and bigger. Of course. The fish Dad lost was a giant leaping out of the water, shaking the fly from its mouth. Us girls became professional canoe paddlers.

Dad looked up from poking a stick in the fire and with a smirk on his face, saying, "Since it went so well today, you can change spots in the canoe for tomorrow's trip."

Our mouths dropped open as Pam and I looked at each other… "What?!" Not only had we had lived to paddle another day, we evidently merited a repeat performance.

CHAPTER 5

BECOMING BLENDED

Honesty is the first chapter in the book of wisdom.

–Thomas Jefferson

Becoming a mother was always a wish I had as I was growing up. It had a sense of family at its core. Coming from a family of two children, one boy, and one girl, I knew the dynamics of living together with four of us in the house. The hierarchy from top to bottom meant I, the "baby," had privileges different than anyone else. However, many times my brother complained about "How come she gets away with that, and I never did?"

Looking back, he was correct in his evaluation of me getting my way more than he did. The oldest child is the one who typically experiences firm decisions and strict rules from their parents, who are honing their skills at bringing up "good kids." Now add in the differences inherent in raising a son versus raising a daughter.

What my brother Rick didn't realize was that once he left home, I was still "the baby," and a girl besides, in our parents' eyes. I would say the same things to Mom and Dad: "Why did Rick get to do that when he was my age?" Rick never got to hear the answer: "Because he's a boy." I guess as a girl, and as the last child, I needed more protection to stay safe. It was the sign of the times.

Staying "the baby" was definitely not what I wanted to do! For sure! But my opportunity in being the second and last child in the family gave me insights with a learning curve. My parents tried their best, instinctively knowing how to guide us while we were growing up. I still have "Wisdom Stones" that worked for me as a child, and later for me as an adult.

It can be challenging to discern the truest parts of wisdom inherent in the values or creeds we hold close to our hearts growing up. We tend to repeat what we see and do in our original family, and every family is different. But even as children, choosing love, rather than fear, helps us live a life which will set us free!

My firstborn was a boy. Tyler Holden had dark hair and big brown eyes like me, but otherwise he looked just like his Dad. He was a true gift of love in my life. My mother called him a "loving boy," and by that she meant you could hold him for hours and he would be content. But boy, oh boy, put him down, and he was not happy. Some would call him spoiled. Being a new Mom, I thought his behavior was a tribute to our bonding. It wasn't easy carrying him around on my hip all the time, so I got a backpack that worked perfectly. Once he hit his first birthday and started walking, he remained the loving little boy, always giving the biggest hugs and kisses. And he was Daddy's pride and joy.

My next gift of love was daughter Jessica, born three

years later. With blonde hair and beautiful hazel eyes, she favored her Dad's side of the family. She was the sweetest little girl who filled everyone's heart with immense love. My father and Jessica had an exceptional connection, and it was evident that she was a Grandpa's girl from the start.

I have heard that no two kids are the same, and I agree. How can they be? They need to be loved and nurtured according to who they are and what they need in order to become secure adult human beings. Yes, they need guidance from parents who love them and make the best decisions about the boundaries of rearing "good kids" who can flourish in society. Yet they are also always "their own person." As their mother, I tried my best to have them know that I always loved them unconditionally, even when I didn't like the choices they made. Recalling the way I was raised as a child helped me find my way to lovingly raise my own children.

Growing up, I knew that no matter what I did wrong or however I crossed my parents, it never meant they would stop loving me. I had the same understanding with my own children. Tyler and Jessica were a joy to raise and were very loving to each other, other than the relentless teasing Tyler did to Jessica. OK, so I guess teasing was a trait he came by naturally, inheriting from my family genes!

I loved them both to the moon and back. But all our lives were about to change! After twelve years of marriage, I had decided against staying together as a family and filed for a divorce. This was the most difficult and challenging thing I was going to put my children through, for them and for everyone else that the decision touched. Only time and forgiveness from those I caused emotional pain would heal the wounds of divorce. Did I make the right decision to leave? Yes. What took me far longer than it should have was to forgive myself for making this decision, and for my part in creating a broken marriage.

Single parent stories arise from deep wounds in the mind of those who live on. I said many times to myself that divorce was hell here on earth. When you are in the trenches all alone, and your children need guidance from another point of view, life can be very hard. But I was fortunate. Having my Mom, Dad, and brother living near me and supporting me was a huge blessing. In fact, they were my saving Grace. Grandpa and Uncle Rick stepped in many times to help with a fatherly influence during my children's early teen years. Tyler and Jessica also treasured the close relationships and love they shared with both Grandmas.

When dating, I felt I was on a treadmill of memories with past experiences I did not want to repeat. Yet I knew I had this unconditional love that I grew up deep within me to share. I wanted to learn never to repeat my past choices in a mate. Eventually, I stopped focusing on what I wanted in a man. Instead, I began to realize that I wanted someone who could match and accept the ocean of deep love that I wanted to give back.

So, after two and a half years of being single, I went to my knees on a Monday morning. *"God, if you want me to have someone in my life to share my love, then you pick him. I'm done looking. Even if it takes thirty years for someone else to appear, that's OK, because You are enough for me!"* Then I let it go. A weight lifted off my shoulders. The words I heard were, "It will be OK."

Then it was Friday night of the same week, just four days later, and I had had a hard week at work. I was glad I only had Saturday morning to work before the weekend started for me. The phone rang.

It was my friend, Carol. "He's here!" Carol said.

"What do you mean, he's here?" I repeated.

"That guy Roger and I told you about—he's here at the restaurant. Get dressed and come join us so we can introduce you."

Ugh, I thought. "I'm exhausted, and don't know if I want to put effort into meeting anyone tonight," I confessed. My thought went on to *I'm done looking for guys, and God knows I'm willing to wait longer than four days.*

"Oh, come on!" she urged, with a tinge of disappointment edging into her voice.

"OK," I replied, "I will stop out, and I will try to be pleasant, but I'm not staying long." When I walked into the restaurant, my friends were sitting at a table for four. Roger did the honors of introducing us. Then he waved over a waitress to the table.

"Have a seat, Pam," said JJ, the new guy. "May I order you a glass of wine?"

"Sounds good to me," I answered. "Roger and Carol have told me about you, and I thought I would stop by to meet you tonight here at dinner, but you didn't join them," JJ explained. "Glad you could make it after all."

"So sorry," I acknowledged, "it has been a long week, and the snowy weather was a factor. You are right; I usually do have dinner with them on Fridays." The glasses of wine arrived, and everyone toasted each other.

"I'm glad you decided to join us!" JJ said while toasting me.

The conversation went around the table, easily touching on what we had in common as friends, likes, and dislikes…sharing our family stories.

At one point, JJ paused and directly asked me, "What are you looking for in a relationship?"

Wow, I thought, talk about getting right to the point! I looked him straight in the eyes, saying, "I'm looking for a guy who wants to have fun and enjoy a Saturday night out, but is willing to get up on Sunday morning and go to church with me." So there, I said my truth! A little risky, because I didn't know where he stood on that issue.

But JJ sat back in his chair and said, "Well, I graduated from Christian High." Right answer. At least he could understand my faith and my commitment to its importance in my life.

I stayed longer than my first plan, which was to leave early. JJ and I exchanged phone numbers, and I said my goodbyes all around. It took him until Sunday night to ask me to dinner on Tuesday evening.

I met him at the restaurant. I was not letting any guy into my home or the lives of my children at this point. We enjoyed each other's company. We talked about the same things I had given up to God that I wanted so much in a relationship. Again, I straight-forwardly spoke my truth, not just telling him what I thought he wanted to hear.

I realized my voice had, for the first time, a certain

confidence and clarity to it. I heard myself speak what is essential from the core of my beliefs. We left that evening feeling different about each other and continued the conversation and dinners together.

Soon it was Christmas Eve. We went together to his church service; our girls met each other for the first time. Time passed; winter was in full swing, one day at a time, and then it was February. JJ had a large family, and every February, they all went skiing for a weekend up north. JJ wanted me and my children to meet them there. He knew I was always a "package deal" of single woman plus kids. I was a family of three; so was he. It was a huge step for us, but it felt like the timing was right. We gave our relationship time to feel secure.

We loved being together, creating fun and adventures wherever we went. There were many group dates with the kids. But we never gave up our Friday date nights just for us. One evening, we all went out to dinner. We walked into a restaurant, and one of the children put our name in for a table of six. Then when the hostess announced, "Bradys, party of six," the children stood up laughing at the reference to the popular TV show. Other people waiting laughed too as we all stood and started walking towards the table.

All the kids shared a great sense of humor. Four teenagers can come up with the craziest ideas to entertain each other!

In total, I was a single parent for six years. After dating for two and a half years, JJ and I married. Aimee, Scott, Tyler and Jessica stood up as our witnesses, and Aimee and Tyler signed our marriage certificate. I had finally found my soulmate in JJ. I counted my blessings to have a husband who, when I said, "I love you," always said," I love you more!" We were creating a new family with four children. Blending them into a new family could have been difficult, but JJ and I fully embraced the challenge--and each other.

During the children's teenage years, the respect they had for each other was terrific; we felt so fortunate when we heard stories of struggle about blended family problems. Don't get me wrong; there were spats on occasion. However, forgiveness and kindness were what we tried to model when they had disputes. The children knew deep down that they were loved by all their parents, "steps" or not. JJ and I were a united front, showing our children what unconditional love felt like from us. We continually showed them what a successful marriage looked like, as well.

Blended family life, for me, was waking up every morning with a sense of completeness.

READER REFLECTION: UNCONDITIONAL LOVE

What does it mean to you?

The stories I shared in the previous section were snapshots of the childhood that shaped me. I was fortunate in having many moments in early life in which I experienced unconditional love. Experiencing unconditional love in our early life—even sometimes—is so helpful! It leaves an imprint that we can access, if we choose, throughout our life. With memories in which we innocently trusted that we'd be nourished and cared for, a secure inner base is formed which allows us to reach out to explore other relationships and the world as we grow.

Humans are certainly not perfect, however, and even the most well-intentioned and loving parents are bounded by personal limitations and the understanding of their times. Many parents raising children now, for example, would not leave them alone at an ice-skating rink or limit hunting trips to only the boys in the family. But children don't need perfect parents; they need "good enough" parents, and parents are good enough when love underlies their decisions and their children are wise to it.

In this section and in those that follow, I offer you the "nuggets" and "Wisdom Stones" that have helped guide me. They've given me excellent guidance along life's path, so I want to share them with you. I hope you will ponder how they might support and guide you in your own circumstances.

"Wisdom Stones" of Unconditional Love

Love is a currency, like money in a poker game. Love leads you to put in all your chips at once and say, "I'm all in!" because nothing else matters, win or lose. Or you can be the person sitting at the table with a pile of chips, strategically calculating every move in order to win at the game, leaving nothing to share. The only currency that God recognizes is love. Use it for good. Everyone you love will be waiting for you when you reach the other side.

Love is best when it is T.R.U.E. love! T.R.U.E. love, at its best, involves TRUST, RESPECT, UNITY and EQUALITY.

- *Trust* that the people you love also love you.
- *Respect* for everyone, for who or where they are, even the parts of us that are still "in the rough" and not perfectly polished.
- *Unity* that brings life into a full circle of belonging; creating safety.
- *Equality* that manifests as we care for each and every one who has a beating heart.

Unconditional Love and You

Even in the most challenging times in life, most people can recall a moment when they felt unconditional love. It might not have been in your family, but perhaps a neighbor, teacher, or peer shared with you in some way a glimmer of hope with unconditional love. What are some of your memories of feeling loved unconditionally, just for being you?

When does your own heart feel like you are playing "all in" in your current life? It could be times with a favorite companion, whether animal or human. It could be when your heart goes out to others far away, motivating you to find a way to help them.

What does it feel like when your own heart warms to another? What feelings do you notice that are a part of that unconditional love? Very likely, you'll notice subtle "flavors" swirled uniquely into your love for specific others—more tenderness and protectiveness for a child, for example, and more pride or gratitude for a partner or friend. What can you tell about the qualities of your unconditional love for those in your life? Are you "all in" and is it equally being returned to you?

Do you need more unconditional love in your life? It has been said, "It is in giving that we receive." This is also true for love.

Part Two:
LOSS

CHAPTER 6

LITTLE LIVIA

If you can't feed a hundred people, then feed just one.

—Mother Teresa

Albania, a communist regime, had been overthrown by a democratic party in 1992. Many economic hardships had controlled the population in the country. In the capital city of Tirana, there were sparse supplies at the hospital and significant needs for the abandon children living in orphanages. Bethany Christian Services in Grand Rapids, Michigan, was one of the very first into the country to help bring aid and care for the children, especially newborns, then later for children up to the age of three years old.

A call came from Bethany, reaching out to The Bouma Corporation for help: "We need to build orphanages that can properly care for these children." JJ and his brother Doug took up the challenge and went to work making plans to build a safe place where children could thrive, not just survive. JJ worked with the new government on purchasing the land where three new Group Homes would provide better living conditions. He also hired an Albanian architect to oversee the project.

It took well over a year from breaking ground to opening doors at the new facility on the outskirts of town. Fresh air and beautiful grassy hillsides were a very different environment for the children, most of whom had been living in crowded cities.

JJ and I, along with Bethany Christian Services team, had traveled to the dedication ceremony of the first new Group Home that would house the children. An American foster family had been chosen to oversee the care of the homes and children, and had committed to a year's stay, and possibly beyond. It was ultimately the start of open adoption proceedings between Albania and the United States.

Looking out the airplane window, we saw a small building that was next to the airstrip. No other planes were parked on the ground. One lone car, an old white Fiat, was at the end of the runway. When the plane touched down, then slowed at the end of the runway, it turned towards the building. The car drove in front of the plane with a sign attached to its trunk. It said, FOLLOW ME...in English.

I was glad to have landed safely. I looked at JJ with a smile, knowing this was another adventure we were about to embark on together. He just smiled back at me, knowing what I was thinking.

We deplaned on the runway, then grabbed our bags and walked into the building where the military soldiers greeted us. They, too, had smiles on their faces, but machine guns over their shoulders. We were aware of this country's suppression from outside influences, as they were under communist rule for a very long time. Still, it was as if we were stepping back in time to around the 1930s.

The van arranged for our pickup and brought us to the home of someone who had once been a high-ranking communist military leader. We were given a bedroom and bathroom to ourselves. It was summer and extremely hot—of course, no air-conditioning. The mattress was on a rope foundation and there was a sheet and feather quilt on top, with two pillows. We were fortunate, being treated as important visitors. The new government understood the magnitude of the outside world, and the need to help rebuild the infrastructure of the country.

The next day was the first day we visited the existing orphanage in the city. It was war-torn and damaged by mortar shells. Entering the building, we walked up three flights of stairs to where the infants were kept. Entering the room, I was surprised by the pervasive silence and feeling of emptiness. I was greeted by the caregivers, who knew we were there for a visit. Smiling, and very proud of the children, they were overseeing the entire room as their jobs. Looking around I saw that lining the walls were approximately 20 iron cribs. All children had a clean diaper on, and I assumed they were recently fed because there were no crying babies.

But something was missing. Something's not right, I kept thinking. I knew the walls had not seen a fresh coat of paint in years, yet there were different colors and patterns that went up the walls just so far. Then the obvious hit me. I turned to the lead team member and asked, "Christen, why are the walls around the room missing paint right at the crib level?"

"Oh, that's from years of children left in their cribs; they would pick paint chips off the walls and eat them."

"It's lead paint!!" I exclaimed.

"Yes, you're right," she said, nodding her head sadly.

The horrible thought of toddlers occupying themselves in such a way created an indescribable scene in my mind. I became aware of a profound physical feeling developing near my heart as I encountered the inhumane belief that orphans in this country's culture were regarded at almost the same level as stray animals in the streets! They were given just enough food and attention to stay alive. Adoption was not something an Albanian family would consider for themselves. With few resources, they only took care of their own. So, orphaned children were housed in institutions according to their age. Once they moved into the mid-teenage group, most left to fend for themselves.

The reality of my heartache was soon to be a familiar feeling for these infants.

Christen introduced me to each caregiver. Then I was asked to pick out a child to care for during the dedication ceremony the next day. We were bringing all the babies to the ceremony, and there would not be enough caregivers to hold them, so my help was needed. As I walked along the line of cribs, I felt like we were picking out a puppy to play with, not a human being, so tiny and frail. Rounding the corner of the room, I heard a screeching sound. Not a cry, but a sound like an injured baby owl calling for its mother. I stopped at the crib.

"That is Livia," said Christen. "Would you like to care for her tomorrow?" She picked her up and laid her in my arms before I could answer. "Livia is nine months old." My arms felt like I was holding a newborn. "We weighed her, and she is at 11 pounds right now."

I gasped for air. "What is she getting fed?"

"Every baby gets four bottles a day, two diapers, and then is held once," Christen sighed.

"Yes, I will care for her tomorrow, but I want to tell you right now, this schedule of care has to change!!" I said, in my instinctive "Mama Bear" voice. "That's why we are here. It's all about the children!"

Christen squeezed my arm with understanding.

The rest of the day we spent touring the capital city. It was very interesting. Tirana was the hometown of Mother Teresa, so we visited the Sisters of Charity compound, and met the widows and nuns caring for them there. I felt very privileged for the opportunity to witness such love for some of the least of these.

JJ had brought back the plans of the future children's homes when he had visited the job site while construction was going on, and I had seen them. They had turned out beautifully! However, there were a few finishing touches needed on the first home before the children could move in, which would take a couple more weeks. So, we would take the children to the new Group Home for the ceremony, but then they would return to their world of iron cribs for now.

The day of the ceremony was a pretty big deal. The Prime Minister gave a speech on the opportunity to care for the children of the country. Afterward was a reception with all the people who had made it possible. Livia had been cradled in my arms the whole time; sleeping through part of it. I found myself thinking, *how can I let her go when this is all over? She needs to be held and loved!!*

I knew the foster family would be setting new guidelines on the care the children would receive and would foster the health and emotional growth needed for them to thrive. But will it be enough, I wondered?

"We need to take the children back to the city now," said the driver. I walked out to the van as two caregivers were taking the babies from us, one by one, and laying them on the floor of the van. On their backs, all in a row—what?? *There is NO WAY you are taking her from me; she is mine!* I thought. The words were swirling in my head. *This child is not riding on the floor in the back of the van!! I'm going to hold her myself!*

JJ stood next to me. Reaching out, he very tenderly took little Livia from my arms. Then he put her down on the floor next to the others, and the van door closed shut. My eyes were not just filling up with tears; tears were running down my cheeks and hitting the collar of my dress. "This isn't fair!" I sobbed. "That's why we are here, Pam. It will get better. I promise." He put his arm around me to lessen the ache inside my body.

It would be almost two years before I would see Livia again.

Once home, I pondered. What could I do to support these children and give them a chance for a better life? I needed to go back. As I made plans to return, I learned that I was returning to a place that had gone through some growing pains and changes. The children were now thriving, and the caregivers were learning how to love others and nurture the children. Nutrition and healthcare had greatly improved by people's commitment to ongoing donations and support from back home.

I saw the needs first-hand during my first visit. Now, I stockpiled dry goods, toys, and essentials such as children's books. I was determined to go back and thank everyone who had made it possible for the children to grow and learn.

I had told everyone I knew in my community about what was going on in Albania, including my physician. I also let him know that I wanted to take a trip back.

"When are you leaving?" he asked.

"Six months from now; would you like to join me?"

"Yes!" was his answer.

Well, the project grew from there. Other healthcare providers and teachers wanted the opportunity to help make a difference. Dear friends wanted to hold babies and contribute to the Group Homes success! A team of eight of us went, all of us loaded with two suitcases, each weighed down with seventy pounds of donated goods still not available for purchase in the country. An industrial washing machine and dryer had been shipped via crate cargo when the homes first opened. However, they needed a new motor for the washer. So, I packed it in my luggage.

We arrived safely, but what a difference I found when we landed! The airport was bustling with regular flights coming and going. They even had a metal scanner in place, so everyone put their bags through, then went outside the glass wall to retrieve them. It seemed odd to go through the scanner while coming into a country instead of leaving one. I was the last one to place my bag on the belt to be scanned. My military greeters were there, just as before, with machine guns on their shoulders. Only this time, my bag sounded off the alarm because of the metal motor. I immediately grabbed the handles of the bag, as did the soldier. He started yelling in Albanian, and three more soldiers instantly showed up.

Again, I was the only one speaking English. It might not have been smart, but I would not let go. It was indeed a tug of war! I knew the importance of that motor and the value it would bring on the black market. There was no way I was giving it up without a struggle!

I started yelling back, just like the soldier, only in English. I had learned a few Albanian words before, but not enough to carry on a conversation. I tried to explain it was for the orphanage, and it was a motor, not a bomb!

Still hanging on for dear life to my bag, it dawned on me to start throwing names around. The first one that came out was the Prime Minister. I put my other hand to my ear like I was making a call to him. Things changed after that. The soldier let go, and I was allowed to go through to the other side with my hand still clutching the handle of my bag. I guess "Mama Bear" showed up again, defending our precious children in need! My knees didn't stop shaking until an hour or so later.

Our team was very excited to see the children and the progress that had been made in two years. As for me, I just wanted to set my eyes on baby Livia. When we entered the door of the Group Home, the children were all playing in an area with toys. The foster mother knew about Livia and my connectedness to her. She was now two years old, and still very small, but, oh, it was so good to see her happy and smiling! It was a heart-filled moment I will never forget!

"I'm so glad you arrived today. Livia will be leaving the orphanage tomorrow." Wait a minute, WHAT? I had just got here. I want time with her again. Time to love and play as a mother would with a two-year-old, to read her stories and rock her to sleep!

"Her mother is coming back to take her home. She could not take care of her when her husband left; that is why she has been here. Her new husband has agreed to raise Livia as his own now," the foster mother explained.

My thoughts went from great sadness to jubilation, all in a second. The chances of Livia being left behind in the orphanage for years was very real. The opportunity of being brought back to her family told me that the love her mother had for her never wavered. Nor did every prayer I said for little Livia for two years. I experienced love coming full circle for a child who was never mine.

Livia taught me how love and loss are the two sides of the same coin. Many times, I have imagined her smiling up at me, encouraging me to always carry my coin with LOVE facing up.

CHAPTER 7

ALS

I don't want to sit and wait to die. I want to live until I die.

—JJ Bouma

JJ and I had been married ten years. It was just after Christmastime when JJ started to have a scratchy voice and cough after a severe cold. Up until then, he was never sick—in fact, he was one of the healthiest people I had ever met. So off to the doctors we went to get his symptoms checked out. After several months of no definitive answers, our doctor ordered a CAT scan and EEG muscle testing for JJ.

It was Friday afternoon, and it was a beautiful fall day. That meant heading up to our vacation home in northern Michigan for a relaxing weekend, enjoying the changing of colors on the leaves. We had been looking forward to a break from the stress of medical visits that just left us with more questions.

JJ's doctor asked us to stop by the office before we left. We were eager to hear the results and the details of a treatment plan that would finally get him better. The doctor walked into the room with a very stoic demeanor...we wondered why, but in the next moment, we learned why. We heard the unbelievable words: "JJ, I'm very sorry to say this, but you have a probable diagnosis of amyotrophic lateral sclerosis, or ALS—Lou Gehrig's disease." At that moment, the air sucked out of the room, and I found I had no breath. We looked at each other and knew what it meant — a death sentence. We had watched our pastor Ed Dobson struggle with ALS for five years, and he was going to be retiring from the pulpit on Sunday as this cherished role had become more than he could do. Russ Hibma, a dear friend and Vice President with The Bouma Corporation had a daughter, Brenda, who was also battling the disease. So, we knew what we were facing.

There was nothing for me to say to the doctor, so I just listened when he told JJ to consider getting a second opinion. I felt like I was in a very long tunnel hearing voices from way far away. The doctor was telling us to go home and be with our family and friends and share this news of "no known cause" and "no known treatment to extend your life" with our loved ones. Our future was gone. All our dreams were gone. We had planned to travel and spend time up north, boating and snow skiing with the family. We had planned to savor together the fun of watching our grandchildren grow up. But it felt as if our future had evaporated into nothingness.

The only clear thoughts I had nudged me to begin focusing on how we were going to handle JJ's challenges-- a vibrant, loving, and successful businessman, husband, father, and grandfather who was only 53 years old, now faced with inevitable decline. I searched deep within me, wondering how I would support and love him through the next two years that we hoped he had left.

We left the doctor's office, and JJ threw me the keys to the car and said, "You drive." As I slid into the driver seat, I placed my hands on the steering wheel to stop them from shaking. Looking up at the bright blue sky, I silently said, "OK, God, this one is too big, I need your help." JJ and I both had a solid faith. It was what truly brought us together. Now, I drew on this faith like never before.

"Where do you want me to drive?" My voice cracked asking the question. "Go to the lake," was JJ's answer.

My in-laws lived on Lake Michigan, so we headed there first to share our news. Shock and great concern were on both their faces, and we knew it would take time to process. So, we continued on to visit our children. JJ needed to be with them and to console them. Even then, he comforted everyone with his signature line, "Everything will be OK."

We continued to call on our extended family and friends throughout the weekend to share the news. It was hard for everyone to accept, including us! In disbelief, we grasped at straws and looked for a different diagnosis. We decided to contact Mayo Clinic for a second opinion the following week.

Sunday morning came. We went to an earlier service at church than usual, arriving before the start of the next one.

"Let's go in the back entrance. Maybe Pastor Ed will be there in his office," JJ said. "I want to tell him about my diagnosis and say goodbye." We stepped in the door, and there was Pastor Ed walking straight towards us in the hall. His head was down; this was his last day to teach the love of God to the congregation. Then enter early retirement.

"Pastor Ed, can I talk to you for just a moment?" JJ asked. Pastor Ed stopped, then looked up at us. JJ gave him our news: "On Friday, I found out I have ALS." Pastor Ed waved us in, saying, "Please come into my office!" After we shared the short version of details, Pastor Ed asked if we could meet on Tuesday and visit further. We did, and the meeting was the beginning of a soulmate friendship—the kind of bond when you can finish each other's thoughts and words. It was no longer a pastor-parishioner relationship. It was two brothers with the same disease, and a calling to love God and love others!

It was hard for everyone to accept, including us! We both felt exhausted. We were, I think, on autopilot. But I realized that while we had talked with everyone else, yet we had not talked about *us*! "*What about us?*" my heart was crying out! I had a sense JJ needed to be the one to start the conversation, so I waited. Our turn finally came one evening when we returned home from sharing our news with so many.

Sitting in his favorite chair, staring at the television straight ahead in silence, he then spoke, "I don't want to sit and wait to die. I want to live my life until I die." The flood gates finally opened up! We held each other and sobbed our hearts out. It was the defining moment for us. We shared every thought we had ever wished we had said but left un-said. We found the place of knowing that no matter what, you have each other's back.

We were in this together, and we each knew it was going to be the most magnificent adventure of our lives and not just an ending of a story.

JJ was CEO of The Bouma Corporation, a family-owned commercial construction company. Monday morning came, and a meeting was scheduled for all employees to attend. JJ stood firm, explaining his future, and then stepping down from daily operations. I stood by his side, and he squeezed my hand, telling everyone in the room, "My life is on warp speed now, wish me well." There was great applause, with tears streaming down so many faces. JJ was loved and respected by so many!

One of the best descriptions of JJ was that he was a big thinker, and adventure was his middle name. Previously, the company had built three orphanages in Albania when the country left a communistic regime. Later, we hosted Albanian business people in our home in the United States. Wherever there was a call to help others, we always opened our doors.

Now it was time to plan the year that was ahead of us. The second opinion confirmed an ALS diagnosis, and the disease would run its predictable course, giving JJ two to five more years at best.

First, we went to the Holy Land and climbed mountains with Pastor Ed and his wife Lorna. JJ had always wanted to visit The Church of The Holy Sepulcher, the Wailing Wall, and be baptized in the Jordan River. We went to an area of the river that was not visited by tourists—fast running glacial water with rocks and rapids. JJ waded into the water with his close friend, Ross, who had, with his wife Terri, also joined us on the trip. Standing on a large boulder in the river was Pastor Ed, perched above the waterline. "Don't let him float away, Ross!" Ed said, laughing out loud. "Hurry up, Ed; we are freezing in here!" Ross yelled back. Even at such a sacred moment, we all laughed so hard!! It was a moment that had such meaning, and yet the light-hearted banter was what we all needed! All said and done, JJ and Ross came out dripping from being completely immersed from the baptism. "That worked out great!" said Ed, laughing even harder. "Now get me off this boulder before I fall in." He faired very well, and even kept his toes dry!

Next we took all of our children, their spouses, and grandchildren to a tropical island to create more memories in the sun. We spent days surfing, sunbathing, and making sandcastles together. JJ asked everyone one day to come gather together and listen to what he wanted to say to them before the disease took away his ability to speak. When you face a terminal disease such as ALS, it allows you to be the most open you have ever been with your family—telling your loved ones what they mean to you, and what you hope for them in their future without you. It is a choice each person decides for themselves, which can be difficult for some to speak their truth. It freed JJ to let everyone know how much they meant to him. It also let the ones who listened to his words take in the depth of love he had for all of us. I learned the importance of saying and showing, "I love you!" without needing anything in return.

One of the things JJ had on his bucket list was to drive across America on Route 66. "What do you think of this one?" he asked, dropping a Corvette brochure in my lap. "A red convertible would be a perfect ride for the trip!" JJ said with a big smile. "Sweet car," I replied. "Is that the one you are thinking about?" JJ smiled an even bigger smile. "Yes, I will pick it up tomorrow!" he said. *OK then, here begins another adventure*, was my thought!!

We were a part of a group of friends, that we called ourselves "The Adventure Club." They heard about our trip and said, "Let's all go together." "OK! Get yourselves a corvette then!" JJ, chimed in. "Let's bring attention to ALS and raise money for the new clinic I want to build here." *Clinic?* This must be another adventure I haven't heard about yet, I thought! We had to travel two and a half hours to receive supportive care at the University of Michigan, so a clinic closer to home sounded much better. "So, what are your thoughts on this clinic you want to build?" I asked when we were alone. "I won't be here to use it. It will be for everyone else who will be coming after me with ALS," was JJ's answer. I was not shocked.

Raising $66,000 on Route 66 became the goal of working along with The ALS Association and so many friends and family, giving their time and fundraising efforts to succeed. Ten weeks later, we were in a caravan with 13 corvettes, two motor homes, and a film crew who came to capture the moments. We visited eight other PALS (people with ALS) en route, crossing eight states to bring attention to this cruel disease.

Pastor Ed came along to be the voice for JJ, who was struggling to be understood when speaking now. But his signature "thumbs up" said it all. By the time we arrived at the Santa Monica Pier in California, the group had raised $326,000 for the start of the clinic. This success was a measure of how JJ did most things, exceeding expectations, always thinking about others, and making a difference in so many lives, with his kind and giving spirit!

ALS takes away so much. It causes nerve cells to break down, which means that a person's body eventually no longer belongs to them, but to the disease. Its impact spreads beyond the patient, and close loved ones often feel like they, too, have surrendered their lives to the disease. Why it attacks certain people but spares others is unknown, and the seemingly random onset of ALS feels especially cruel. Nevertheless, JJ lived through all this with his loving nature, courage, and generosity intact. Ultimately, he found a way to make even ALS give back— fulfilling a deep desire of his heart.

CHAPTER 8

THE PRESENT: GIFTS OF A CAREGIVER

For it is in giving that we receive.

—St. Francis of Assisi

The emotional side of dealing with an elderly parent, sick child, or terminal disease is a bit of a moving target. The two stories in this chapter come with the "Wisdom Stones" about what it is like to remain in the Present, even when flooded with memories of the past and questions about the future.

In late life, my mother struggled with heart and breathing issues. My father took on the caregiver role for the last three years of their sixty-year marriage. When I received a call from him one day, it changed everything. "Hello, Pam, it's Dad. I wanted to tell you that Mom's not doing too well, and I think she needs to go to the hospital." Then silence from his end of the phone.

"OK," I said, scrambling to infer what was going on. "Do you need to call 911 right now, or do you mean she needs hospice and breathing treatments that you can't do for her?" I'm sure my concern came through in my voice. Again silence. "I can't take care of her anymore," he eventually replied. I could tell he had to sit down in a chair to let out a sigh. The emotional load of care had brought an end to what he could physically give her. He was now depleted.

"Does Mom know you are talking to me right now?" was my next question.

"No, but I need your help and support to have her understand hospice would be the best for her," he said. I could tell the words were difficult for him to say.

"I know, Dad," I reassured him. I'll drive up to be with you. It will take me a couple of hours. Don't worry, you both will be just fine. I will call Rick and he can meet me to help, too. Just keep doing what you can, and we will see you soon."

It is difficult when elderly parents don't live close to you and they need extra health care. But they did their very best, on their own terms, for many years. I packed a few clothes, then JJ and I took the two-hour drive. My brother Rick arrived shortly after us.

"Hi, Mom," I said, as we came in the door. "I thought we would come up and visit for a few days. How are you feeling?" My words were upbeat and positive.

"Oh, pretty good," she replied. "It's tough for me to breathe, and Dad can't do the treatments like at the hospital." So, she was thinking exactly like Dad. It may be easier than I think to get her into emergency care, I thought.

"OK," I said, calmly. "I'm going to talk to your doctor and get you *and* Dad some help." As I left the room, I looked back at them. Dad was sitting on a chair next to the bed where Mom laid resting with a bank of pillows under her head. Neither spoke aloud what they needed to say to each other; they didn't have to. They just needed to sit together and hold each other's hand, understanding that the time left might be very short.

The ambulance driver wheeled Mom into the emergency room. Her doctor was expecting us. They gave her the breathing treatments she needed. Then the hospital admitted her. The decision was that JJ and I would stay near the hospital, and Dad and Rick would drive back to Mom and Dad's house, just out of town from the hospital, then return in the morning.

Mom was so frail. I kissed her good night and said, "I love you, Mom."

"And I love you twice as much, sweetie." She had not called me that since I was four years old. As it turned out, they were the last words she spoke to me.

In the morning, she stayed asleep due to the medication. We didn't think it was her time to go yet. We were waiting to speak to the hospice director to make arrangements for her transfer to the care facility later that afternoon. After the director left, Dad, Rick, and JJ also left to take care of some business across from the hospital. I expected it wouldn't be long before their return.

I found magazines to glance through on the table. I pulled up my chair next to Mom at the head of the bed. When she woke up, I wanted her to know I was right next to her side. It was tranquil in the room, and an article in the magazine held my interest.

A few minutes passed—I'm not sure how long—and I looked over at Mom to see if she was awake. I noticed a soft light filling the room, as if someone was turning the knob on a dimmer switch up very slowly. I looked around to see what it was and then back at Mom. There was a glow around both of us, and she had stopped breathing. I stood up then and watched as life left her body.

The glow of soft light was not from the window. The draperies had been drawn shut. I needed a nurse to see this! I ran out of the room and down to the nurses' station. "Please come and help; my Mom has died!" Running back into the room, I stopped cold. The glow in the room was gone. Mom laid so peacefully in the bed. The nurse who had followed me back checked her vitals, then came and put her arms around me and said, "She's gone."

"OH, I cried, "you don't know what this woman meant to us as a mother and wife and friend! If only I had one inch of her love and character." The tears flowed, and I couldn't speak anymore. Losing a parent in their later years is somehow accepted as normal and expected. But when it happened, and I was actually in that moment, I experienced a profound acceptance of Mom and gratitude for her living a full life. I never questioned why it was her time to die.

Little did I know, as I accepted the end of her life, that I would be given an opportunity to see her leave her earthly body, and it was beautiful.

The immense sadness of loss my family and I felt in losing Mom was a preview, I later realized, of me assuming the role of a caregiver in the near future. Just one year after Mom's death, JJ and I were facing a diagnosis of ALS.

During the last six months of JJ's life, the responsibility of feeding tubes, wheelchairs, and using a talking device to communicate rested on my shoulders. Twenty-four / seven...but those are just the days and hours. A caregiver counts it in minutes, and sometimes seconds. Time gets lost in the aloneness of care.

I was lucky: family and friends came and gave great support to both of us, many times over. I remember the ones that came often. Others who visited once or twice were just as important.

I figured out during those times that "God only knows" what I was going through. But I also came to realize that He was filling me with the Present of His spirit. And here was where I learned to *stay in the present*. I never allowed myself to think ahead to what my life would be like when this was over. I needed to respond to everyday changes so I could help us both live the life we chose together—in the present. Nor did I have any insight into how I was going to respond to the road ahead named ALONE.

It was three days before Christmas. The tree lights were glowing, and all the ornaments were placed perfectly. The gifts were under the tree; the grandchildren's toys were ready to be opened. The doorbell rang, and I went to answer it. Pastor Ed had stopped by just because he was in the neighborhood. "Hi, Ed, what a pleasant surprise! Please come in!' I took his coat and then heard my mother-in-law calling us to come to the bedroom.

Ed and I walked into the room together. Ed, Sharon, my brother-in-law Doug, and I watched JJ take his breath for the last time. "That's how I want to go!" Ed softly exclaimed, watching his friend pass away from a disease that would eventually take him as well. Peace filled the room, and we all knew we had witnessed a beautiful moment with JJ as he left his earthly home.

It was fifteen months after we had heard, "It's ALS." So little time, but JJ had always lived his life at WARP speed, for sure, always making a difference in so many lives, with his kind and giving heart! Did he walk with the faith and the knowledge of where he was going on to from here? Yes!

The ALS story was an event in both our lives, but I was the only one who survived the disease. I survived because, unlike JJ, I had a choice from the beginning. I chose to live the time I had with JJ to the fullest and doing so was the greatest gift of all. For me, our life as a couple was never about all the amazing things we got to experience together. It was about loving life and not fearing death with a man who loved unconditionally and accepted the same from me.

The outcome was yes, God did answer the prayer I prayed that day with my shaking hands on the steering wheel, the day we learned of his diagnosis of Lou Gehrig's Disease. And JJ and I were never alone on our adventurous journey of life –and beyond.

Things happen in life, to all of us. We may not have wanted these things to happen, and we might desperately wish they were different. But it is our response to these events that give us an outcome. We can use our knowledge combined with our wisdom to create outcomes that surpass the constraints of the events that happen to us, creating new gifts for ourselves and others.

So, when life gives you moments that take your breath away, choose responses that come from love and not fear. As hard as they may be, if you set your mind and heart to respond in a way that creates more love, I promise you will still succeed at this adventure we all call life!

By blessing others, we created something beautiful and life-changing out of pain and loss. We created the gift of a Legacy!

CHAPTER 9:

LEGACY

If you're going to live, leave a legacy.
Make a mark on the world that can't be erased.

—Maya Angelou

All of us who knew and loved JJ came together to make sure his dream of opening an ALS Center and his legacy would come to fruition.

Many meetings with the board of St. Mary's Hospital, including Mary Free Bed Hospital and Michigan State University, began to fill my calendar as the Center came into view. Then more financial commitment was given. We were getting closer to the goal.

The way an ALS Clinic/Center functions is to provide care in one location in the hospital. The disciplines/departments it takes to care for a PAL—a person with ALS—involves a three to five-hour office visit for them. The team of professionals coming together to care for the Pals in the Center is a group of exceptional human beings. Each one of them is an intricate part of the success using their specialty. Respiratory therapists, dieticians, mobility issue specialists and therapists, social workers, and specially trained doctors and nurses.

A PAL's energy depletes through the visit. It becomes more and more taxing on them and their families with each meeting, depending on how long they have been battling the disease. The advantage of receiving care in one location all at one time is immeasurable!

After JJ passed away, staying involved in order to see the Center open was a mission for me. I was making sure to keep my promise to him, thus fulfilling his wish to care for others coming behind him. Statistics show every thirty minutes, a person gets diagnosed with ALS, and every thirty minutes, a life is taken by the disease. So, I knew that the need was great.

I was the only layperson volunteering in the Center when it opened. People asked me, "why are you coming here every week to face this disease when you don't have to experience the pain anymore?" My answer was always, "This isn't about me; it's about families like mine that will learn of their diagnosis today: "It's ALS."

There were times when staff struggled with their own overwhelming emotions while serving a family; they had grown close to in their care. I was that person to put my arms around them when they came back to the conference room. Once a nurse said, "I can't keep doing this, we can never cure them," with tears running down her sweet face.

"Yes, you can make a difference," I assured her. "Stay in the present and remember right now, in this place, this is about them, not you. Use the gift you have, compassion to care for others, and it will get you through." Many times, I met with spouses and family members and listened, to their journey story. They could trust in my understanding when I shared why the Center was here for them.

Staff lovingly named me "The Board Lady," a title which I held for the first eight years of the Center opening.

We all shared a central conference room where we had a dry-erase board on the wall showing who was in what examine room at what time. Each staff member was followed with a designated color magnet. Playing this version of "Who's on first and What's on second" made it fun! It helped everyone to stay on schedule, which was our top priority. Staff knew I was just fine staying on schedule. There was no justification for wasting any time. They knew how precious time was to each PAL and family, and they knew I had lived the story. Efficient, timely care made a huge difference.

I also immersed myself in the knowledge of ALS, a disease that most know as Lou Gehrig's disease. Moving closer to a cure in the past seventy years or so hadn't happened. For me and others, the goal was not only opening the Center for care but finding a cure!

Dr. Deborah Gelinas was chosen as the founding Director to captain the ship. She had many years of experience as a neurologist in research trials. Her mind was brilliant, and her commitment to finding a cure was a real passion. She was always helping the team understand the possibilities of making a difference.

In the world of ALS, Dr. Deb's reputation was global.

"Pam, I have to speak at the ALS World Symposium in Milan, Italy; would you like to go together? There is so much to learn about the work around the world. It would be an opportunity to experience on a different scale the other physicians' and scientists' involvement in their communities." We had become close friends since her move to Michigan. Both of us being single allowed us to spend time together outside the hospital. Aloneness is real on many fronts when you are touched by this disease.

"Yes! I would love to join you!" I said, knowing it was going to have an aspect of adventure I hadn't had for some time.

The seas parted, as you would say, when she entered the room of colleagues. Over the four days, we were together as every other presenter clamored to have time with her, in order to learn more about the ideas she shared. After attending the Symposium, I knew the clinic indeed had the right Director at the right time, making a difference in so many lives, including mine. The education I received didn't come in a book. I sat at the foot of a mentor and soaked up knowledge and wisdom about the world in ALS. I will be forever grateful.

The ALS Center opened nine months after JJ's death. Mercy Health - St. Mary's Hospital in Grand Rapids, Michigan, and now serves over 400 families a year battling the same disease, helping them face the same trials we did, closer to their homes.

READER REFLECTION:
LOSS

What does it mean to you?

Rain laid its healing powers on the land during the night. The sun rose, even though the clouds kept it covered from sight. We needed that rain, as my neighbor would say. The corn is on schedule to be knee high by the Fourth of July.

Something happens in these fields every year that amazes me. It's the march of the turtles, coming to lay their eggs in the fertile soil. Our marsh is a few acres away from where they are called to deposit the future generations of themselves. Many turtles are so old, they have moss growing on their backs. Is this the place they were born? Are they back to repeat the cycle? The farmer's turning of the soil for planting makes an ideal place for nest-building. The environment is perfect for hatching, with the sun warming the earth.

This morning I watched a mama turtle return to the marsh after laying her eggs. Gosh, I so wish I could slow down like her and move with the assurance that I can accomplish my day's mission, whatever it is. Though tired and empty, with only an inner a promise that she did what was asked of her body, mama turtle laid her eggs in her nest, then stepped on to continue the cycle of life. Mother Nature would take it from there.... and she was fine with it.

Seasons of Grief...and Renewal

After a season of grief, it can be very hard to get moving again. But we may be more alive than we feel! Did you know that turtles don't actually hibernate for the winter? If you live near a pond, you may see them moving around under the ice. While their metabolism is at a very low ebb and their hearts are barely beating, they are actually attuned, even while sleeping, to detect the returning warmth and lengthening light of spring. Then they get moving and come up for revitalizing food and air.

Has your soul been spending its days in a cold, dark, quiet place? Does it feel like your spirit is barely breathing; its heart is barely beating? That is nature's way of enforcing rest. But lift your eyes...do you see a glimmer of warmer light? Do you sense the almost undetectable but inevitable return of Life? Some days will still be cold and cloudy, but you can begin to open yourself to Love that surrounds you. Open yourself to nature, too, and let her take her course. Spring will come!

As the season for egg-laying approaches, the mama turtle doesn't come out of the water all at once. With eggs maturing inside her, she spends a little more time on land each day, scratching and sniffing the earth and finding just the right path out of the pond and to her nesting spot. There, she'll use her strong hind legs to create a hole that is just the right size and depth for her eggs, then return to the pond, sink into the mud, and rest.

Just like the mama turtle, you'll sense when and how you want to rejoin the dance of life. You'll find that parts of you have grown stronger. You'll journey on—but know that you, too, will need times to return to your home, absorb your new experiences, and rest.

Loss and Listening

Loss often renders us speechless. Like a pond in winter, the time of silence spills from one day to the next. The beat of our own tender heart becomes barely audible. There's nothing to be said. Yet our minds and hearts are often full—too full.

When we find our tongue again, we may lament, "Why? Why me?" We may feel a sense of unfairness that even leads to bitterness: "Why not her? Why not him, instead of me?" While it is important to let our experience of loss make itself known to us, there comes a time when we must examine what we are saying to ourselves and determine its helpfulness.

We must also listen to what we are saying. How powerful are our words! When we stay fixed on a person, event, place, or ourselves, our spoken words will reflect the state of our mind and our being. The good or the bad. The yin and the yang. And the words that we speak are as sharp as the sword.

From Loss to Love

Loss often involves a feeling of being stuck, a feeling of standing still as the world goes by you. Each and every day, the mind replays what happened. When I have found myself there, my prayer is, "Dear God, bless me and bring healing and balance to my complete being…physically, mentally, emotionally and spiritually…thank you, amen."

Prayer still saves me from myself and my losses of those whom I have loved. Through prayer, I connect, and I no longer feel as if I'm in the tiny boat alone and drifting away from everyone I held dear, and everything I held to be true.

I look back on my times of loss and I see that God was preparing me for now. In this time, this place, I am called to do His work again… and His work is called *unconditional love!*

The stories I shared in the previous section were snapshots of loss that shaped my own adulthood. Through experience, I discovered a truth. As painful as it is to lose a way of life or a loved one, it opens an opportunity for us to learn this lesson more deeply than before: We cannot love anyone or anything more than ourselves. So, we must learn to love ourselves unconditionally!

Unconditional love—even unconditional love for ourselves—is easiest when you have a soulmate filling you with the same love. Unconditional love is the toughest and hardest when you feel unseen and unknown, or when the people you try to give your love will not or cannot accept the depth and the trueness of your gift. When these things happen, you can be left with the feeling of trying to fill the bucket, but there's a hole in the bottom that keeps draining out the liquid balm that has the ability to heal beyond measure.

Even so, the commandment to love each other—as we love ourselves—is the One true universal law given to all of us. So, find the hole that loss left in your bucket. Bring light and love to see where and how to repair it so that your bucket becomes whole; then fill it with healing liquid balm. The wonder of it is that the unconditional love you store up for others will, by its nature, heal you. One of life's greatest gifts is the chance we have to experience and understand the vast and wonderful grandeur of the emotion of love—for ourselves, and for others!

"Wisdom Stones" of Loss

T.R.U.E. loss optimally includes elements of TRUST, RESPECT, UNITY and EQUALITY.

- *Trust* that the pain of loss is part of a healing journey that each person walk alone.
- *Respect* for each other's feelings; no assumption that you know what it is like to walk in their shoes.
- *Unity* when family and friends share compassion—just being there together.
- *Equality* in realizing that no one is exempt of loss. But it gives us a chance to learn from each other and share our love.

Loss and You

The life event of each loss, whether it's a child, a spouse, a family member, you will respond accordingly to all the emotions that come with it. Your circumstances will never match anyone else. The feelings you have will ultimately give you your outcomes. Right now, do you see yourself as the survivor, the victim, or the ostrich who is not accepting the reality of loss? Or maybe all three?

As you stand alone, what would you say on top of your own mountain to the rest of the world? Would you want to scream it out? Sing it out at the top of your lungs? Or sit in silence then give up the weight of loss to the Universe? Remember, no one will feel your loss like you or react the same!

Loving memories are there to go with you. Memories of your loved one are complete--never to be compared or replaced by memories created with anyone else. What memories of your loved one do you hold most dear?

What memories still make you feel loved as you bring them to mind?

What memories do you have of yourself giving to others from a place of love? What do you feel now, as you recall those memories?

What do you know about how to be truly loving to yourself? What practices and daily routines help you best support yourself lovingly?

What will you sense when it is time for your body and spirit to venture out again? How will you know that your heart is stronger and ready to love again?

Part Three:
FORGIVENESS

CHAPTER 10

FINDING FORGIVENESS

Forgiveness is not an occasional act. It is a constant attitude.

—Martin Luther King, Jr.

Forgiveness takes action, not just thoughts or pretending like something never happened. Forgiveness involves taking a step out of oneself and admitting wrongdoing or releasing another for the same. Forgiving can be the most difficult when it is yourself whom you need to forgive. However, I want you to know that whether you have built your walls for protection or physically placed yourself behind them, you can step out from behind them.

    My mother was wise beyond any book smarts I learned. She seemed to float through life with ease; never a scream or holler, but when she used my middle name, it meant I'd better "listen up," as my dad would say. The other attention-getter she had was nicknamed by my children as "the Jessie finger!" NO, it wasn't her middle finger... it was her pointer finger! And it had a long, perfectly shaped nail at its end, and she used it effectively to take the floor.

"I'm sorry...now listen to me," she would start. Then would come the instructions on a life lesson of some sort. "What do you say, young lady?"

"I'm sorry," spoken with true penitence, was always the right answer. It wasn't amusing growing up, but looking back now, I realize it created a habit of saying what you need to say much more straightforwardly. My children would giggle at the finger, and Mom couldn't keep a straight face herself. She had a wonderful sense of humor with the kids. However, the respect and love they had for her was beyond description. Mom was a very remarkable woman who knew how to be resilient, decisive, and tender in one fell swoop, while leaving no enemies in her wake.

Looking back on her life, I believe she lived in continual forgiveness. She never seemed to hold a grudge. She lived by her favorite one-liner, "If you don't have something nice to say, don't say it."

I found forgiveness in my mother.

Adulthood brought me to a time and an issue that I had to learn to address. The issue was my critical view of others, and it perplexed me. I found myself ruminating about why this person or that person did something to another in a hurtful way. Or the classic, taking something out on someone because they had a bad day or were angry at someone besides the person whom they were taking it out on. I was preoccupied with others' unfairness.

Life, as I knew it, involved bedrock values of respect and apologies if needed. But when I found myself in an unfair situation, I wanted to avoid conflict. Instead of facing a battle, I would go silent, not using my voice to be part of the resolution. Often, I said "Sorry!" just to appease the situation. But not taking responsibility for my life and my own reactions caused a problem. The picture of what life should look like in my head wasn't sustainable.

I found that forgiveness is not always two sided. Some streets have a sign that reads, "Caution! Dead End Ahead." As an adult, I had made choices in my life that I thought would lead to happiness. However, when it became clear to me that my course was a dead end, I realized that I didn't want to continue on the path I was on.

Happiness is a place where, no matter what, you can be content. It's not about having it all and waiting for Prince Charming to ride in on the white horse. If someone who looks like Prince Charming or Lady Godiva comes along, be assured that it's a fairy tale, and yes, he or she will fall off their steed at some point—several times. Yet contentment is worth aiming for.

As the decades passed, I realized that I wasn't happy with my life story. It wasn't horrible. I had two beautiful children and a loving family I grew up in and where I still belonged. I had a reliable roof over my head and many friends who stayed in my life. Yet something big was missing and I puzzled about it a lot. How can this happen? I wondered. What am I missing here? What do I need to achieve the experience of living happily and being loved for being me?

When I finally looked within myself, I realized that the baggage in my life was very heavily laden with unforgiveness. This realization was immediate and clear--like a movie playing my life up on the screen. As I saw myself, I was not proud. It was painful to see my role in that movie and realize that it wasn't Oscar-worthy. I felt ashamed…until I heard, "You will be OK, and I have plans for you!"

It's hard to portray what a turning point this was for me. But after that moment, I was truly happy in *myself*. Trying to make life happen was over. Now I realized that moving forward into the future was no longer based on my own imaginary timeline. I couldn't literally see the future of course. But the ability to dream, and visualize the future was something I could do in technicolor! I could do this, and not feel responsible for how or when it would come true. But I had to seize the moment if it materialized in front of me. The movie that I watched the second time became a different script—a separate cast of characters just right for my new life story. Yes, I let myself be the co-star of a life far beyond what my current circumstances showed me.

I found happiness in the action of forgiveness. It was a gift to myself and also one that I could share, while knowing my internal wellspring would never run dry! I could forgive from a place of thankfulness for a life filled to the brim with unconditional love. I could forgive while being grateful for listening to the promise that set me free–from me!

Creating a blended family took effort. No one can expect utopia! What worked for us was a stable and united front on parenting together. Neither parent was ever allowed to be disrespected by any of the children. We each had a similar view of how raising our children would be handled. Yes, there were differences with how we approached each child according to personality. All of them had a different bend to life. Fortunately, the lineup of four teenagers made building relationships easier than expected.

When they made choices that resulted in natural consequences for them, we never changed the outcomes for them to ease their way. Instead, we let them experience the consequences, they had earned, whether pleasant or disappointing. We were both clear: they had to do it themselves, but we made sure they knew we were there for them with advice, when asked, and parental opinion along with some insight when things didn't go as planned.

All the children knew we were never going to keep either one of us from them, creating jealousy. Nor would we try to take the place of their other parent. As parents, our united front showed them no matter what we never engaged in talking against the other parent. Even when the children themselves had critical things to say about another family member, we changed it around to focus on "how we do things in our home."

I believe each child cherished being part of this family of six, even after we became empty nesters. Even then, it continued to take united effort on the part of both of us to maintain the balance of the family unit. When misunderstandings or hurt feelings arose, I found forgiveness to be an act of love. Forgiveness was part of showing our children how to live life by creating a successful marriage for them to witness.

I felt grateful for what we had created, and was proud of our achievement, too. At last, I was living the life that I had known was possible. When a life-changing illness changed all of our lives forever, it brought up again the questions: WHY?? WHY ME? WHY US?

My conversation with God went like this: "You told me You have a plan! You gave me more than any gifts that I could have envisioned. Now you are going to take this man away from me and the love we share! You told me your plan was for GOOD. Now, what?!"

I kept hearing, "It will be OK."

"Teach me what You want me to learn, then!" I'd stop the ranting—for a while.

There were times throughout our next fifteen months together when a wave would wash over me. It would knock me down and land me on the side of the road, stuck in a ditch in my mind. I didn't like it there, either. I learned to make my way back to the present moment, where the love that still filled us was deep and peaceful. The mind cannot hold two thoughts at once. So, once I caught my breath, I'd chose the better thought of the two.

My response not only helped me; it helped us to deal with the inevitable loss for the children. I learned that it takes a different timeline for each one of us as we face the loss and the grief we carry internally.

After the loss of a loved one, clocks stop ticking and tell you no time. Days run into nights, and then it starts all over again. Life is ever-changing; however, in the experience of loss, we unconsciously feel that stopping the clock means we won't forget our loved one. You stay in the same place, sleep in the same bed. Eat at the same table and keep pictures everywhere to remind us of our loved one. Some never change their life again, in reverence of the one who passed. Some go out the next week and choose to refurbish their life with everything new in order to relinquish the past and move into the future. Neither of these ways of coping are better than the other. They are just a couple of ways the timing of grief plays out. It's different for each person because it's personal.

Not one size of loss fits all. Grieving is not even the same for everyone in a culture, like one in which a widow must wear the veil over her face for a certain number of years before surfacing to live life again. Maybe psychologists have an idea about how much time must pass before the person should say to themselves, *yes, it's OK to come out of hiding now*. I, however, believe every widow and widower has an inner clock that runs on their own wisdom. If they listen, they can sense the pace that's right for them.

However, if you feel stuck, like time is standing still, then talk to someone. If you have similar feedback from many people close to you, give heed. If many people say they are worried about you, talk to an expert. If many people are hinting that you can live a new life again, pay attention.

Your new life experience will begin a new chapter in your life story. Your new chapter will not be the same as any in the past. You can leave guilt, pain, and un-forgiveness behind as you turn the page; all the "would-have, should-have, could-have" thoughts won't work. The new original story you create will be about YOU and

LIFE. You'll bring along the best pictures of your MEMORIES, and you can choose to take these with you always.

I learned forgiveness in myself by following my wisdom and setting myself free to accept the plan for good that was waiting for me. Forgiveness—forgiving life, as well as forgiving yourself and others for any missteps—makes space for you to love yourself again. When you make that turn, you will experience deeply knowing that YOU ARE ENOUGH

I have found it helpful to remember this simple, ancient Hawaiian forgiveness prayer.

HO'O'PONOPONO

I'm Sorry.

Please Forgive Me.

Thank You.

I Love You.

CHAPTER 11

LIVING LIFE

What we have once enjoyed we can never lose.
All that we love deeply becomes a part of us.

—Helen Keller

The opinion of others can weigh heavily on you after the loss of a spouse. It did me. Your family and friends want to help you, but they might not see it through the same eyes until they have experienced becoming a widow or widower themselves.

Compassion and empathy are beautiful gifts that cover it all. I was very thankful for them, believe me! But until you have "walked in my shoes," the depth is something hard to understand.

My doctor suggested I attend a support group of widows and widowers six months after JJ's death. A couple of widowed health professionals who had later married held group meetings in their home, Susan Zonnebelt-Smeenge and Robert De Vries.

They had written two books on the subject. *Getting to the Other Side of Grief: Overcoming the loss of a spouse* and *The Empty Chair: Handling Grief on Holidays and Special*

Occasions. Why was I there? I was there because I needed a litmus test, of sorts, to see if my mind was on the right path to accepting singleness. There were about thirty of us in the room.

I have to say, after listening to others' stories I realized that ALS involved an aspect of grieving a loved one that was different than others. One widow in her thirties lost her husband to a car accident; she had young children. Everyone in the room felt the heaviness of her grief. Another widower had battled his wife's cancer right alongside her for several years. She rebounded and everyone hoped for recovery several times. But ALS doesn't give you a possibility of survival, even if all the medicine in the world was available; it would only prologue the inevitable. It is a final diagnosis. It's a diagnosis that tells you, *this is it*, and this is the path you will end up taking.

I learned a great lesson that evening: my grieving began when I heard JJ's diagnosis of ALS. So, by the time he passed, I had been in grief for all most two years. Hope left me long ago. So, my grief had begun much earlier that family and friends who didn't really accept JJ's fate until he died. Why? Because I had experienced minutes, days, and hours of watching the decline. In our own family, few were older than me and had been widowed.

I did learn something valuable that night in the group with others like myself: the path that I chose to heal from my grief would set the trajectory for the rest of my life.

Since I was, at that time, in my early fifties, I realized how short this life could be. Time was no longer frozen and had started moving again. But I realized that the clock had started to tick again in a very different way.

Living alone allowed me a new companion: a puppy, a standard black poodle who was the sweetest ball of fur! I gave her the name of Lucy. When I left and returned home from an errand, I would walk through the door and sing to her "Lucy, I'm home!" in my best Latin accent from the *I LOVE LUCY* show! Oh, the greeting of a "happy to see you" face made the emptiness of the house drain away! Pets are such healers here on earth when aloneness reigns.

Lucy gave me something else to be responsible for; she took my mind off myself. The saying of describing dogs as "man's best friend" is correct. Dogs never have an opinion on our life; they live in the present, only knowing how to love unconditionally.

The children still came every Sunday for pizza night supper, a tradition begun and sustained from when we blended as a family. It was the highlight of my week!

I traveled with some friends and went out for dinner and activities when invited. I started to realize that at my age; it was a couple's world. So being the first to be widowed in my circle of friends felt odd. It felt odd not only for me, but for them too. For some, it wasn't easy to be around me. Maybe I represented what their lives would be like when their wife or husband passed away.

I heard comments like "I'm going first because I am not going through what you just did." When I heard them, I would smile to myself, thinking, "Honey, you have nothing to say about who goes first." I understand wishful thinking, I do! It's hard to see the suffering of someone you love close to, and nothing changes to relieve the pain.

When I started to date again, some family members accepted it, and some didn't. I went to counseling to better understand the dynamics. I now realized that life had changed for all of the family. JJ and I had been unified parents and missing his presence, for me and the children, was a considerable loss.

My counselor tried to get me beyond what was a regular pattern for everyone—supporting me with the validation to create a new life and a right to LIVE AGAIN. I began to see that I would never leave my family behind, but I could feel for another again. I could find another person that could share my life adventures.

Yes, I went to the place I had gone before, asking God for a mate. I asked for someone that could love me for *me*, and who could understand the depth of my loss. Then I released my desire, because I had accepted where I was in life and was feeling happy again. I was doing things I liked to do when I was young. Hunting and fishing were my favorites. Trout Unlimited was an organization I supported, and I attended their meetings.

Ten days after I released the shortlist of who would fit into my life, John Miller came on the scene. He was divorced, then married the love of his life, only to lose her to cancer. We are the same age. His favorite things, growing up, were hunting and fishing. John has the same strong faith that I do and came from an upbringing in a family similar to mine.

The handiest of handymen, I would put him up against the best! He has an intuitive understanding of things. One of his favorite lines is "I get it."

Again, I call his arrival in my life another "God thing."

Visualization, the art of seeing your dreams as real, works when it is for your good—every time!

We started dating two years after JJ and John's wife, Julie, had passed away, within just three months of each other. We dated for a year, then became engaged, and six months later we married.

John's work took him to China each year to check on the company he worked for and the plant operations. So, the first three years of marriage, I traveled with him, with the opportunity to have a driver and interpreter during the day while he worked.

One of my hobbies is photography, and it kept me very busy. I loved visiting all of the architecture and Chinese gardens. The flowers and trees were exquisite as well as tranquil. The koi ponds were teeming with fish, and I so enjoyed watching the grandparents caring for their grandchild. Capturing photographs of the young and old in China was such a pleasure.

I didn't realize, at first, how much the Chinese people found me to be an oddity. I was American, but I'm also two heads taller than most of the population in the country! Many times, I was stopped, and parents or grandparents gestured for me to get my picture taken with their children. They were always holding up the peace sign with their fingers. I asked my interpreter one day what they were saying to me in Chinese. She said, laughing, "They think you are a basketball star from America." It made me laugh, too.

John was an avid hunter, and early in our relationship, he never missed a deer hunting season. I so enjoyed his stories of this or that hunt. It felt so much like when Dad and I would talk, and I was the little girl wearing his red wool hunting jacket. One day I explained to John the story about how I was never allowed in deer camp because it was for boys only.

"What?" John exclaimed. "You can come with me to my family's farm, that's where I hunt. Opening day is coming up this weekend; do you want to join me?" I think I ran out the door right then to buy my license. It wasn't a tag on your back to wear, but orange now was the color of the season. John put a blind in the woods beforehand with a couple of chairs, and a heater for warmth was ready. I was up at 4:00 am, excited to walk out to the woods in the cover of darkness.

"OK, you will get the first shot if a buck comes through," John offered. We agreed on it. And so, we waited together. Sitting quietly in the woods can be very entertaining. Every little animal is rushing around collecting food for the winter; quite comically at times, offering plenty of entertainment even when you are sitting stock-still in a deer blind in the cold. The sun finally came up; it was a beautiful fall day with sunshine and a cool breeze.

"Look out this side of the window," John said in a whisper. "Get ready you are going to take him." A beautiful nine-point buck was limping towards us.

I waited for the shot; it took just one to lay the buck down. "Nice shot, Pam!" John's voice raised.

I unzipped the blind and said, "He dropped right there," pointing in the direction of the rack lying on the ground. Talk about adrenaline—we were exhilarated to see the magnificent animal.

John's son was also hunting in the area and came over

to see the action. "Wow, very nice," was his remark. We noticed the deer had a large gash in his leg.

"It's good we could take him. He probably wouldn't have lasted the winter," I observed. Both John and his son agreed.

John gave me the instructions, "Pam, you stay here, and we will walk back to the house and get the cart to carry him back."

"OK," I said, starting to choke up.

I sat down on the floor of the woods, and all sorts of thoughts were starting to go through my mind. It was 10:30 in the morning, and all I wanted to do was call my Dad and tell him my story. He was in an assisted living facility. His hunting days were over.

Luckily, I had enough signal on my cell phone to make the call. "Dad, guess what?" I said when he answered his phone. "Do you know what day it is today? It's opening day of deer season, and I'm calling you to say I just shot my first buck! I'm sitting in the woods with it right now."

"Oh, honey, tell me all about it!!" he exclaimed. As the tears rolled down my face, I had my hands on this deer who gave his life. Now I was telling my Dad that all my life, I had wanted to go hunting with him, and now was so grateful that I got to share my hunting trip with him.

"Will you thank John for me for taking you? I wish I could have been there to see it!" His happiness for me came over loud and clear on the phone.

Rules of life changed quite a bit over fifty years, when that little girl wasn't allowed in deer camp as she had always hoped. But I was so thankful my Dad was still with me to experience his daughter in a deer camp where it wasn't just for boys anymore!

To this day, John and I continue to create our adventures. We even fulfilled his top bucket list trip of trout fishing in the outback of Patagonia, Argentina. Again, I was the only woman fishing out of twelve of us. But it didn't matter. One of the fellas' fishing in another boat said, "You are keeping up just fine. Every time I look over at your boat, you had a fish on the line!"

John replied proudly, "You and I go fishing, but Pam goes catching!" He was laughing out loud with pride. I kept up with them smiling more than once or twice, and fishing camp made for a beautiful and memorable trip together.

Life goes on. I have chosen to live it and enjoy it to the fullest. My memories continue!

CHAPTER 12

SPIRITUAL GIFTS

When you find your spiritual gift, God will give you the opportunity to use it.

--John Maxwell

I had been waiting for the email, eager for the seminar dates to finally being posted. Now, it was time to register. I had read Jack Canfield's book, *Success Principles,* four times; I had also read his *Chicken Soup for the Woman's Soul* multiple times. Each year, in a week-long event, Jack shares and teaches the excellence points in his workshop, Breakthrough to Success.

My excitement mounted as I hit the "send" button on my computer to complete the registration. I felt so grateful for the opportunity to have five days with all the beautiful people from many countries, cultures, and professions who would come. Together we'd study the Success Principles that are now taught around the world.

I met Khursheed on my very first day of the seminar. She was standing in the lobby at the water bottle filling station with her arms full of several copies of the book she had just finished writing. Now in print! Her beautiful dark hair and glowing skin spoke of an ethnic culture that originated far from my own. I told her that I was presently writing my book, and from that morning on, we clicked right away. We met for dinner that first evening.

Over dinner, I learned that she was a very accomplished woman. She held a doctorate in Human Science, and this was not her first time attending a Jack Canfield seminar. We spent hours sharing our lives, hopes, and dreams for the future. We developed a kinship/friendship that felt like we had known each other for years, and could last a lifetime.

The next five days proved to be everything and more that I had come to learn. Every day was filled with teachings of Success Principles, designed to be able to go out into the world and make a difference at home, the workplace, and the community. We were asked to change seats around the room and meet new friends at breaks and lunch every day. Many of us would exchange business cards to remember names of those we met and where they were living. On the back of my card, I had put the story of "The Wise Woman's Stone." The gift I shared with others was a heart-shaped red jasper stone to carry in their pocket, reminding them of the wise woman's story of Unconditional Love.

The week went by too fast. There was so much to learn, and so many people yet to personally meet. As I was finishing up a conversation in the lobby with a group of attendees that where sharing their experiences of the week, I glanced over to see Khursheed walking into the ballroom where our final dinner of the seminar was being served. "Khursheed, save me a seat, will you please?" My voice, I'm sure, sounded like I would never see her again!

"Sure thing," she said with a casual wave. "I'll see you inside."

When I entered the ballroom, I realized that there were over fifty tables filled with hungry people. How in the world was I going to find her in this sea of humanity?

I glanced across the room in hopes I could spot her, but with no luck. I decided just to start walking to the back of the room. I looked to my left and my right, hoping for the sight of that beautiful head of long black hair. All the way at the back wall, I spotted her in a group of people I had not yet met. They were all talking and laughing. I assumed she knew them from past seminars.

Upon reaching the table, I set my plate down, pulled out the only empty chair, and said to Khursheed, "I wasn't sure I'd be able to find you."

"Well, here you are," she said. "I saved you a seat next to Rhonda." I introduced myself to her and the entire table, as I had throughout the conference, "Hi, everyone, I'm Pam from Michigan."

Rhonda invited me to have a seat and commented on the delicious offerings of food. A tall girl like myself, Rhonda had a distinct sound to her voice. Strong and yet friendly. My guess was she was about half my age. I noticed she had a profoundly engaging way of listening to the conversation going on at the table. I unwrapped my silverware from my napkin and settled into enjoying my dinner.

"Pam is writing a book called *Un-doing Conditional Love*," Khursheed announced to everyone. I smiled and wiped my mouth with my napkin, momentarily shy to have the spotlight suddenly thrust on me. Khursheed went on. "My book is about Conditional Love, it's so interesting how we both came at the subject from opposite views."

The gentleman sitting to her left said, "Khursheed, your book is amazing. I have had a chance to read some of it this week."

Chiming in myself, I added, "I also was gifted one of her books and I agree—it's amazing."

"Thank you so much!" Khursheed said. "I am pleased with sharing my voice to help others do the same."

Rhonda was sitting between us and seemed to be content with not joining in. Yet she made me feel like I should be asking questions about her. I turned to my left and looked at her, then said, "So, what will you be doing when you return home as your work?" I asked. I noticed she sat up straighter in her chair.

"I am a healer and medium," she said with a slight smile. "I help those that want to reach the spiritual side and connect to their loved ones." She said this with a very calm voice as she put down her fork. I immediately sat up straighter in my chair, too, knowing she was the first person I met this week with a story this different!

"How did you start doing this work?" I asked, suddenly wanting to know more. Never have I met someone who seemed so sure of her gifts. Her answer came, "As a child, I was made fun of for telling stories that no one believed until they came true. Or see things like angels or loved ones who had passed on," she said, picking up her fork again and starting on her dessert. I was sure my mouth was hanging open. My own fork was lying on my plate. I could feel the questions swirling through my mind.

"Do you think that some people have experiences similar to you, but in a much lighter fashion?" I asked. "I mean... maybe feeling the sense of Presence of something or hearing words of wisdom when no one is there." I could tell by the way she looked back at me that I had captured her interest with my inquiries.

Rhonda took a sip of her wine before placing it back on the table. She looked me straight in the eye and said, "I believe that everyone has a guardian angel and I've found that most people have experiences like that, but they can't always remember."

Rhonda was as normal as everyone at that table; a professionally well-dressed woman with perfectly styled hair and makeup. She was not a fortune teller with a crystal ball, rubbing on it until things appear. I am describing well educated gal, confident in her conversation, and someone didn't have to prove or hide anything from anybody. She had spoken her truth.

Because I was the last one to be seated at our table for dinner, most had finished their meals before I did. Looking over at Rhonda, I asked, "How is your dessert?" As she took a bite of the chocolate cake, it crumbled and fell down in her lap. We both smiled and agreed it was well worth the frosting that left a smudge.

The DJ turned up the music, and Khursheed said, "Come on, let's dance." But my feet hurt too much since I wore heels for the evening in order to be more dressed up.

"No, you go ahead. I'm not finished with my dessert yet," I replied.

The noise of the music made it harder to hear each other. After watching the group dance for some time, we both agreed it wasn't our scene. As we stood up from the table to leave, I said, "Very nice to have met you, Rhonda, and I wish you well and great success in your business endeavors." She smiled and said the same.

As I left the ballroom that night, I wondered if I had just experienced another "one of those moments," when I just knew. I call it "a God thing." Rhonda's life story was very different from mine...or was it? As I left the ballroom and walked back toward my hotel room, I started to get that certain feeling I get...

That night, as I settled into bed, I thought back on the numerous moments when I've felt a certain something. Maybe, just maybe, I thought, what I experienced was a sensation of the Presence that stays with me and lets me remember and recognize these moments.

In the past, I would say to myself, with uncertainty, "What was that?" Then I would hear the words, "You will be OK." Something would brush by me, and I would notice the soft breeze. That's when I would say, with no hesitation and a smile, "OK, I get it."

I've had always wondered how many other people have had the same experiences at least once. I asked myself, "Am I different than most?" Or maybe is it because so many of us are different, and fear to share our spiritual experiences.

Explaining is not easy when you get the raised eyebrow and a dismissive answer, "Oh, really." I think it's easier to wait upon the nudge I get before I share my stories. Then I usually hear, "I get it...me, too." They often speak softly, as they look around for the "Oh, really," ones to overhear them and make a dismissive comment.

These experiences are real, surprising me in the moment, and coming from the spiritual side of my life. They happen to me, and I've learned to celebrate them. Fear or evil doesn't exist there. Instead, I experience God's presence and gifts to me: UNCONDITIONAL LOVE, protection, and peace.

It's just a glimpse of what is in store...when I leave my earthly body!

CHAPTER 13

KNOWLEDGE + WISDOM

The future belongs to those who believe in the beauty of their dreams.

—Eleanor Roosevelt

Looking back on my life, I realize that I have been so blessed. I had a family who loved me unconditionally even when I made mistakes and learned from them. Looking back on all I have shared with you in this book, I hope you've learned from some of my mistakes, too. I also hope you've seen that life is rich in abundance, and no matter where you are in your life story right now, opportunities await you.

The opportunities I had in traveling parts of the world embedded in me that the God of this Universe is much larger than the church across the street from my elementary school. Oh, He's still there, for sure! But experience has taught me more. What did I learn? God is everywhere *I Am*.

On the tops of mountains, I've climbed and returned from the deepest valleys of this earth. God was there. At the Wailing Wall, I wrote prayers on a little piece of paper and then stuffed it in the cracks of the wall like thousands of others have done before me. I celebrated a Bar Mitzvah in the Synagogues of the Holy Land. In the Vatican, I looked up at the ceiling of the most famous chapel in the world and sat quietly in St. Peter's Cathedral in England. I was invited into Mother Theresa's Home Courtyard for widows in Albania. I walked into the waters and immersed myself in the Jordan River. I stood next to the spires on the roof of The Duomo in Milan. I even found myself in the Confucius Temple in China studying ancient scribe and on top of The Great Wall.

Never, as a twelve-year-old girl who couldn't pray out loud in class, did I imagine that I would have these opportunities. But God was with me, then, and still is, in the beautiful gift of Spirit.

Some life lessons took longer before I had the ah-ha moment of "I understand now." So, I hope you are patient with yourself if nothing makes sense right now. Perhaps you have lived the entirety of your life in one community. Perhaps you have sought meaning in the clouds above you, and maybe your "cathedral" is made of arching trees shimmering in the sunshine. Even though your experience and my experience may be different, God is with you, too, and as near as his beautiful gift of Spirit in your own life.

I have also learned from achieving my goals that life is waiting for me to set more. Every morning is a new opportunity to right the wrongs of the past and celebrate the "I did it!" moments. Every morning is another start of a day to go after your dreams—whether you are young or old.

Our culture in this country encourages us to dream. The United States was and still represents "The American Dream" to many people who have come and carved out a legacy for themselves and their families. They believed in their dream, worked hard for it, and it was achievable. The possibility to dream in a free country is something I have never taken for granted.

I have taught in countries where dreaming didn't exist. It was an eye-opener for me to experience cultures where Knowledge and learning are the prizes, but Wisdom is not prized as part of the whole.

What is the difference between Knowledge and Wisdom?

Knowledge is facts and ideas that we acquire through study, research observations, and life experiences. Wisdom is the ability to discern and judge which aspects of that Knowledge are actual, right, lasting, and applicable to your life.

Knowledge is learned and is held in the brain; consider it the KEY. Wisdom is felt in the heart as discernments, beliefs, and emotions; consider it the LOCK. The inner guidance system of the heart speaks to us first before our head engages, but its maximum power is only available to us if we tune in and listen to it. Often this is only possible if we find a way to direct our attention away from our brain and into our heart.

We also need to allow ourselves to feel deeply to receive love. For some, feeling has been numbed. It may feel natural to recoil from injury. But stopping the ability to sense intense pain also stops tender and loving feelings that lead us to the inner healing that can free us. The experience of loving and choosing a better life we can dream of is in reach. Opening up the heart to feel again is the action needed.

So, turn the KEY to open the LOCK and let love pour out as your treasure. Only you can create the magnificent gifts of love, in your very own way, that spring from the knowledge and wisdom that life has given you.

My challenge to you is, dare to feel again. Dare to love again. Dare to go beyond your limitations if fear is holding you back. Trust that you will be supported in ways you don't yet understand. Happiness is a gift waiting for you.

As we bring our time together in this book to a close, imagine me sitting next to you and pressing a "Wisdom Stone" into your hand and looking into your eyes with love and confidence. Ask for it, believe it, you then will receive it. Your vision of your life is up to you. *Make it a great one!*

READER REFLECTION: FORGIVENESS

What does it mean to you?

I will always love you. I just might not like what you did!

— Jessie (my mother)

I'm a knitter. Have you known the joy of being able to put two sticks together and creating something you or a loved one will wear someday? It's very relaxing, and also very rewarding.

I use knitting to describe the other side of making mistakes in our lives. In knitting, if you make a mistake, you have to unravel down to that mistake and then reknit that sweater back together. When you're a beginner, it's tough to get every stitch right every time. That's why the work comes out a little crooked. Sometimes it comes out too small or too large; typically, it's because you didn't know how to be consistent with your stitches. Or it's because you didn't want to go back and correct a mistake, even though you knew you made it.

So today...perhaps your life has unraveled, and you want to start your life over. Reknit your story. You can if you want to! With practice, patience, and belief as you work on the project of YOU, you'll create the shape that will begin to fit the person YOU really are. Patiently, you are waiting to wear the new YOU!

How we start is by taking baby steps and being consistent. By thinking and visualizing, and choosing actions, small and large, that fit our vision, we create the life we want and deserve! So, let's get started. Together we will see in the mirror the person YOU have become...and that fits YOU perfectly!

In this section, I offer you my final "Wisdom Stones" that have helped guide me toward forgiveness. I hope you will ponder how they might support and guide you in your own circumstances.

"Wisdom Stones" of Forgiveness

Forgiveness is best when it springs from love! T.R.U.E. forgiveness optimally includes TRUST, RESPECT, UNITY and EQUALITY.

- *Trusting* your heart to feel the depth of the emotion.
- *Respecting* others' views that differ from ours, and lovingly forgiving them anyway.
- *Unity* in facing each other with the gift of an opportunity to forgive.
- *Equality* is realized when forgiveness is a two-way street.

When you forgive someone that has harmed or emotionally hurt you it's a choice to let the event or circumstance go. You may carry it with you for a lifetime, not realizing the act of forgiveness is not for them, it's for you. Finally stand up for YOU by letting go of the memory baggage on your back. It's not your battle anymore. YOU forgive YOU so YOU can live your life free from something that no longer defines you. Rise up and call yourself whole and healed!

Forgiveness and You

What would it be about if you described forgiving *yourself?*

When was the last time you remember going to someone and ask them to forgive you? Was it something that keeps bothering you in your thoughts of some action that happened between you and someone else?

How did you feel after asking for forgiveness, even if the other person chooses not to reciprocate?

The action of asking someone to forgive you is the second step. The first step belongs to us. But apologizing by saying, "I'm sorry," is where most of us stop. We are fearful that perhaps we won't be forgiven. By saying nothing, you deprive the other person of the opportunity of taking in your words of requesting forgiveness and then communicating their forgiveness: "I forgive you, too." Is there a situation or relationship that awaits you taking the first step? Is there someone who needs to hear you say, "I'm sorry"?

When forgiveness is a two-way street, a relationship can be instantly repaired. The communication is now at a healing moment, and precious words can be spoken: "Thank you, I love you." Is there someone whose apology you need to accept?

Remember, taking 100% responsibility for yourself is the road to walk, knowing we can't change how others act or think. All manipulations to make over the ones you love is futile. Show others the changes in you by asking them for forgiveness. Then thank them for the gifts you can receive. Ultimately, "I love you!" is the greatest gift that can ever fill one's heart!!

What are some relationships that need this healing in your life?

THE WISE WOMAN STONE

The story is often told of a wise woman who, while traveling in the mountains, found a precious stone in a stream. The next day she met another traveler who was hungry. The wise woman opened her bag to share her food. The hungry traveler saw the precious stone in her bag and asked the woman to give it to him. She did so without hesitation. The traveler left, rejoicing in his amazing good fortune! He knew the stone was worth enough to give him security for a lifetime.

But a few days later, the man traveled back to find the wise woman and return the stone to her. "I've been thinking," he said. "I know how valuable the stone is, but I give it back in the hope that you can give me something even more precious. Please give me what you have within you that enabled you to give me the stone."

—Author Unknown

ABOUT THE AUTHOR

Pam grew up in Grand Rapids, Michigan, raised by God-loving parents who nurtured and supported her. As a young woman, she experienced divorce and the challenge of raising children alone. While single, she met the love of her life, JJ, but later lost him to ALS. Despite this loss, by loving herself and forgiving life she was able to embrace love and found a new path for creating her life again.

Pam Miller has over 25 years of experience as a business owner in multiple markets. She has worked with organizations and individuals, helping them build their dreams, accelerate their results, and create richer, more fulfilling lives and businesses. Pam has appeared in publications such as *The Grand Rapids Business Journal* and *Greenstone Partners* magazine. She was also invited to speak to the United States Senate Committee in support of the 2018 Agricultural Bill. As a sought-after speaker, Pam offers transformational workshops and seminars to individuals, entrepreneurs, and organizations globally. She is a certified life coach and trainer with the Canfield Training Group and Life Mastery Institute.

In writing this book, Pam shares the path she has walked through love, loss, and forgiveness. Her mission is to bring healing and hope to those who want to be set free from living a conditional life to living a life of unconditional love.

Contact Pam Miller at www.pammillerconsulting.com or www.undoingconditionallove.com

Made in the USA
Columbia, SC
12 April 2021